SLY
EVIL
SHADY
UN-
ETHICAL
DECEITFUL
FRAUDULENT
CROOKED
AMORAL
SNEAKY
CORRUPT
IMMORAL
UNPRINCIPLED
DISHONEST
WICKED
ILLEGAL TRICKY
WRONG
DISHONORABLE
UNCONSCIONABLE
SLIPPERY
UNSCRUPULOUS
UNPROFESSIONAL
DIRTY

UNDERHANDED
UNFAIR

unethical

LIFE IN SCOTT WALKER'S CABINET
AND THE DIRTY $IDE OF POLITICS

ED WALL

LITTLE CREEK PRESS®
AND BOOK DESIGN

Mineral Point, Wisconsin USA

Little Creek Press®
A Division of Kristin Mitchell Design, Inc.
5341 Sunny Ridge Road
Mineral Point, Wisconsin 53565

Book Design and Project Coordination: Little Creek Press

First Edition
August 2018

Printed in Wisconsin, United States of America

For more information or to order books:
visit **unethicalbook.com**

Library of Congress Control Number: 2018951615

ISBN-13: 978-1-942586-43-2
ISBN-10: 1-942586-43-4

This book is a personal reflection on my time spent at the highest levels of Wisconsin government, having served two governors and two attorneys general of both parties in leading three of the most critical public safety agencies in the state.

It is a work of non-fiction and I have attempted to accurately describe events, conversations, and discussions from my memories, notes and other documentation. My conclusions about people, circumstances and actions as stated in the book are purely my own, based on the events as I witnessed them. The observations and commentary shared are my own personal recollections, thoughts, and opinions based on my personal interpretations and experience. I leave it to the reader to draw their own conclusion on the people and subjects discussed.

I dedicate this book to my family and close friends. Throughout this entire ordeal, they stood faithfully by my side, knowing the truth. They rode the roller coaster of emotions that go with hope and defeat, never hesitating to rally to my side. They were a small army of love that lifted me when I stumbled and gave me the energy to persevere. It was only through their loyalty, love, and encouragement that I found the strength to write this book. I am blessed.

table of contents

PREFACE

I have always been a conservative. My ideology has usually been tied to Republican positions, and I've been motivated throughout my life by the belief that we should all go out and earn our way in the world through thoughts, deeds, and service to others.

My work ethic was instilled in me by my father: "Do more than you are asked, better than the others, and faster than expected." Throughout my life, it was that mindset that moved me ahead and caught the attention of the people I worked with and for.

I never cared much for politics or politicians and still don't today, with more reason than ever. They seem like fast-talking con artists who promise everything and deliver little. They claim they are going to make changes that benefit us, and then they get caught up in the deal-making and scheming that suck the ethics out of them like a leech. Their focus swings like a weather vane from public service to getting re-elected at all costs. They morph from righteous orator to parasite in two shakes of a donor's tail. That said, there are politicians I do respect and like personally because they speak the truth and lead with their hearts. I wish there were more of them.

I began my career as a cop. And like most cops I know, I was staunchly conservative, in part because I didn't want the government taking more of my meager income for taxes. But, from a job standpoint, I tended to like Democrats because they got us "stuff" like equipment and more manpower, and they worked with our unions. No matter who would win, though, we would complain. That's how we are. Our jobs create pessimism about our fellow man; we often deal with people at their worst, and they aren't always happy to see us. But we bring order to chaos.

As a cop, you quickly figure out that at some level you are always working for politicians. Your agency heads are appointed by them, and often promotions are given out because of them. The lower down the totem pole, the more insulated you are, and those years at the bottom were amongst the best years of my career. The further up the ladder my career went, the closer it took me to politicians, and the more compromising it became. But at every level, I would convince myself that I could make a difference for the people who worked for me and the people we served. In some cases, I got good things done, and lives were changed for the better. Those are the memories that I hold dearest because the others are too painful to look at. It's like looking at photographs of a car wreck where you lost a loved one. It never gets any easier.

As a state trooper in New Hampshire, I lived by our motto: "Commitment and Dedication, Without Compromise." Unfortunately, I would learn through firsthand experience that in Scott Walker and Brad Schimel's Wisconsin, there wasn't much commitment or dedication, and everything from personal ethics to the well-being of society could be compromised in exchange for political favors, money, votes, ego, status, and, ultimately, power.

When I first saw Scott Walker in his campaign commercials, not knowing who he was, I was somewhat impressed with his "common man" appeal. He seemed straightforward, honest, and motivated. He took his lunch to work in a brown paper bag, as I did. He wore jeans and a sweater, as I did. He looked you in the eye when he spoke to you, just as I do. He was the first politician who had struck a chord with me. I thought, "This one may be different."

Likewise, when I first met Attorney General Brad Schimel, I thought he was a good guy. He seemed approachable, and he was a prosecutor, so he had some understanding about cops. He seemed like a straight shooter. But as I would learn over six years working at the top levels of state government, everything is not as it seems. ♥

TEN SNAPSHOTS

SNAPSHOT 1

Shortly before the election of 2010, I was the head of the Wisconsin Division of Criminal Investigation in the Department of Justice. Milwaukee District Attorney John Chisholm contacted me requesting assistance with an investigation he was conducting into gubernatorial candidate Scott Walker and his campaign staff. On the night before the election, he executed a search warrant on one of Walker's staff members and requested we assist.

Ultimately, the John Doe investigations into Walker and his campaign would attract national attention, and based on my experience as a cabinet secretary, I would realize that the allegations in the complaints were probably true.

SNAPSHOT 2

It's just a few days after Walker was first elected governor, and I came into work one morning and found a rather shabby looking Saturn parked in my reserved (and personally paid for) parking space. I called the Capitol Police, and they informed me that the car belonged to the governor-elect. I replied, "Tell him he has an ugly car. But he can stay there, and I will use another space." I chuckled as I moved on, but there was something I liked about a guy that drove an old, dumpy car and became governor.

When I eventually ran into the governor in the transition office, we had a few minutes to talk. I told him the story of his car parked in my space and my telling the dispatcher to let him know he had an ugly car. We laughed, and then we talked about his thoughts on his new position, and he wanted to know more about what our agency did. It was a pleasant conversation. I remember walking away thinking, "He seems like a regular guy who wants to serve."

SNAPSHOT 3

Scott Walker was a man on a mission who wanted to get himself noticed on the national stage and quickly. On February 14, 2011, scarcely a month into his new position, Walker introduced Wisconsin Act 10, which was ostensibly crafted to address budget shortfall issues. That thinly veiled excuse for the real purpose of Act 10 did not conceal the fact that it was aimed at dismantling organized labor across public sector agencies and fundamentally destroying the unions.

What stopped me in my tracks was not the breathtaking scope of the bill, but the carve-outs that had been inserted. The bill would exempt law enforcement and firefighter unions from the limited bargaining rights put in place for all other unions. The reasoning offered was because their working conditions were unique, and public safety was paramount. Unfortunately, there were glaring conflicts in how that exemption was written. It specifically allowed the Wisconsin State Patrol the right to bargain but excluded the rest of state-level law enforcement. My own agents in the Division of Criminal Investigations (DCI), the Capitol Police, the Department of Natural Resources wardens, and the University Police were all excluded from the exemption and lost their bargaining rights.

SNAPSHOT 4

The capitol was under siege. I deployed our DCI tactical team to the governor's office to assist the State Patrol Dignitary Protection Unit with close-quarter support while Walker was in the building. By this time, there had been numerous threats of violence against Walker and his family. However, the irony of the situation wasn't lost on me. Here we had the governor who had intentionally cut my special agents out of the union protections he granted to other law enforcement agencies being protected by those same people in response to the protests he had caused. I couldn't help but wonder what he thought as my staff, heavily armed with tactical weapons and ballistic gear, were everywhere he looked, protecting him despite what he had done to them and their families. They were professionals, as they always were.

I had many long talks with the DCI staff about Act 10 and the effects it would have on them and their families. Nobody was happy about it, me included. In fact, the majority were very angry. Some of that anger radiated toward me because they saw me as supporting the governor and Act 10 by engaging our agency to assist in dealing with the protesters. As I explained to them, we all occasionally had to do things we did not like in our jobs. I did not share my personal feelings on Act 10 with them because it was not relevant. I had a job to do, and everyone at the DCI had a job to do, and we all needed to be above politics regardless of how we felt. It was a tough pill to swallow, but they understood the situation and pulled together.

SNAPSHOT 5

Your first cabinet meeting is something you never forget. I was nervous driving to the capitol, where the meetings were held in the governor's conference room. That room is beautiful and ornate with wall and ceiling frescos, gold-gilded wood carvings, raised panel walls, and a huge marble fireplace. There was the front table going from side to side, which was the governor's table. Then arranged in a long line of large ornate tables forming a "T" from the governor's table were the secretaries' seats. Each seat had a nameplate in front of it, and I walked around looking for mine. There was an intern from the governor's office straightening the chairs and squaring up the nameplates. I asked if there was a rhyme or reason to the seating for the secretaries, and she replied that the larger agencies sat up near the governor's table. My seat was up near the front by the governor.

As the secretaries arrived, I walked around and introduced myself. They welcomed me to the cabinet with, "Congratulations, Mr. Secretary," and I heard more than once, "Corrections? Good luck."

SNAPSHOT 6

I would learn that the governor's office didn't like communicating internally if it left a paper trail. In fact, they were highly averse to creating any kind of record. That was a frustrating caveat to place on an agency so understaffed and always perched on a precipice of potential crisis. Time and again, either I, my deputy secretary, assistant deputy secretary, or executive staff would be called down to the capitol to do in-person verbal briefings on issues that would have been much quicker if sent by email. I was chastised more than once about sending a note or comment by email because it might create a record. The governor's office was under constant siege with open records requests, and they obviously preferred to reply, "No records matching your request." This was a very distinct culture that every cabinet secretary understood. Was it put in writing? Of course not; that would be a record.

SNAPSHOT 7

Shortly after the governor's re-election, on November 10, 2014, I received information from the Milwaukee County District Attorney's office concerning allegations of staff abuse of youth at Lincoln Hills and Copper Lake Schools, the state's juvenile detention facilities. We needed to try and identify any potential victims and the officers involved as soon as possible. Once we had that information, we would then set the investigation in motion. I asked the Office of Special Operations to take control of the investigation so that people at the institution would not be investigating it themselves. We could not afford to have the appearance of impropriety attached to this because the implications were too big. If this had been going on for years, God forbid, there could be victims all over the state.

SNAPSHOT 8

On the morning of November 29, 2015, I received a call that a youth had been injured the night before when his toes were slammed in the door of a cell room. In the beginning, it sounded like an accident, but as the morning went on, the news began to change. The youth's toes apparently suffered worse damage than was initially related to me. On the follow-up, I was told that his toes were "de-gloved." That meant the skin and flesh were peeled back by the door edge, and that was a serious injury in my book.

I reviewed the video several times, frame by frame, with our Office of Special Operations staff. When I looked at it, my conclusion was that the youth's toes being jammed in the door was an accident. As the officer was slamming the door, which he should not have done, the youth stepped forward and put his bare foot in a bad place. However, what alarmed me more was what happened next. The officer had passed the tether strap, which is connected to the youth at the wrists with his restraints, through the door trap, before slamming the door. This was standard procedure to retain control until the door was secured. The youth would then place his hands out through the trap to have his restraints removed once safely inside.

However, after slamming the door, the officer took the strap and yanked it twice very hard, slamming the youth into the door on the other side. That was not an accident; it was an assault.

SNAPSHOT 9

I spoke to Attorney General Brad Schimel on at least a dozen occasions about Lincoln Hills and Copper Lake, and the need for additional resources. I explained exactly why a thorough investigation was required and the far-reaching implications of the case. We shared everything possible with him and his staff, and yet they still seemed to consider the case to be more of an inconvenience rather than the critical case it was. I began to wonder if there was some kind of agreement between the governor's office and the DOJ to get rid of or water down the investigation. Schimel would claim later, when asked if he should have devoted more resources to the investigation, that "hindsight is 20/20." Hindsight had nothing to do with the case.

SNAPSHOT 10

You never forget the taste of a gun in your mouth. The acrid assault on the senses of bitter metal, gun oil, and tears of anguish swirling together across your tongue as the brain races and the body trembles in protest. The clicking noise your teeth make chattering on the cold steel as you quiver in agony. The cold sweat and tingling fingers, as fine motor skills abandon the body in anticipation of what is coming. Fight or flight. Visions of the people you love, the people you hate, and those you blame flash through the mind like a deck of shuffling cards.

Likewise, you never forget the people and cascade of events that bring you to that deadly precipice where the feeling that ending your life is somehow more appealing than what stands before you.

However, if you are fortunate enough that God steps in and lifts you past that tenuous moment of deadly indecision to survive the mental anguish that tortures you, a stronger person can rise from the depths of despair. But you never forget the horror. The emotions. The cost. The taste. ♥

2

THE BEGINNING

Come with me. I want you to know where I'm from, and how I took this journey.

My family came from a comfortable, conservative upbringing where we had more than many. My dad always voted Republican, but he liked John F. Kennedy because he was Irish Catholic, like us. Our religion was an important part of our lives growing up. We never missed Mass, we did volunteer services with the church, and at one point I was considering the priesthood as my vocation in life. We had our family home in affluent Trumbull, Connecticut, where my parents and all five of their children lived in relative happiness. We also had our summer beach cottage on Long Island Sound in Fairfield, Connecticut, where we spent every summer. So yes, it was a blessed life that we took for granted.

Ever since I was a kid, I knew that I wanted to do something to help others. The things that made the biggest impressions on me throughout my life all seemed to involve people who sacrificed for others. Stories of the saints in catechism class, priests, nuns, soldiers on the battlefield, policemen, firefighters, paramedics: All of those who put others before themselves were so inspirational. I clearly remember when my teacher put me on the Safety Patrol in the sixth grade and helped me put on my orange waist and shoulder strap adorned with that shiny badge. The teacher told me that it was my job to watch out for the safety of my friends and classmates. That feeling of purpose and responsibility never left me, and I knew my path in life was going to be one of service and taking care of others.

Our family was blessed with my sister Susie, who had Down syndrome. I was the oldest and still remember when she was born in the 1960s and the commotion in our house. My dad shared with me years later that when she was delivered, the nurse and doctor told my parents that she had Down syndrome and suggested that they not even look at her, but instead have her sent to an institution. My father quickly told them that their daughter was a gift from God, and they would not be sending her anywhere. Susie came home, and she was one of the greatest blessings any family could have. You see, Down syndrome kids don't know how to hate; they only know how to love.

In high school, I was involved in the vocational agriculture program and was responsible for the equine project, overseeing the school's horse and pony. Right next to the high school was the junior high school, where the special education students had their programs. About once a week, I would bring the pony over to the junior high school and take the special education kids on pony rides. This wasn't a task or part of a curriculum, but an opportunity to see them smile and get excited as we walked the pony in circles, giving each kid a thrill to ride in the little saddle.

As I wrote this book, my beautiful little sister Susie got her wings and returned to heaven after battling Alzheimer's. Despite not recognizing me at the end, her smile never left. Her purity and love had a deep impact on all of our family, and her never-ending happiness will live on in the memories of all who knew her.

When I entered college, I volunteered with the American Red Cross doing emergency blood runs at all hours of the day and night. I still remember the satisfaction of getting blood to those in need, of being just a small part of a team that could save lives through cooperative efforts. I studied for my Emergency Medical Technician (EMT) certification as an elective course in college and became a volunteer on our local ambulance service.

It was an intense experience. Performing CPR, delivering babies, tending to incredible trauma, and having people living or dying in your arms was all part of the EMT job. It was rewarding, tragic, breathtaking, and exasperating all in one. Adrenaline coursed through your veins as the alert tones went off and you climbed into your rig heading off to a situation where you were going to be expected to make potentially lifesaving decisions while others watched. That adrenaline rush, the weight of decisions made in split seconds, and the need to rely on your education as well as your common sense challenged you. It was a challenge I enjoyed.

When I was growing up, law enforcement was an honorable career. We looked up to police officers. They stood between us and our bad dreams. Our parents always told us to trust the police; they were the good guys.

Crime? The police will catch the bad guy.

Lost? The police will bring you home.

Violence? They will protect you.

When the police came in contact with us as kids, we were in awe of their presence. Badges, guns, bullets, handcuffs, and uniforms were the emblems of bigger-than-life heroes.

My father had a successful company that most people around us imagined I would take over when I finished my education. Unfortunately, I never felt the passion for my father's business in industrial tools. My memory of the day I told him that my path in life would not lead me to take over his company will never leave me. I told him that I wanted to be a cop, and I braced myself for the lecture, the anger, the disappointment. But instead, with watery eyes, he said, "If that's what you want to be, then be the best cop you can be. Just be careful." I took his charge not as a challenge but as a tender directive from a man who practiced the simple philosophy that you had to do a job you loved. He lifted a tremendous weight of expectation off my shoulders, and I will forever be grateful for the way he sent me on my career path.

I began taking police exams in my senior year of college while working full-time with a commercial ambulance service and taking a full course schedule. I was fortunate in coming out first on the list in the two police department testing processes I entered. I was offered officer positions in Darien, Connecticut, and Meriden, Connecticut, on the same day. Darien is a beautiful bedroom community in affluent Fairfield County and at that time was the highest-paying police department in the state. In contrast, Meriden was a blue-collar city with the challenges of high crime, diverse populations, motorcycle and street gangs, and below-average pay.

I chose Meriden. Why? Because I wanted to be a cop in an environment that would give me the most valuable law enforcement experience and the ability to make a positive difference in people's lives. I wanted to fight crime. When I accepted the offer from the Meriden Police Department over Darien, many of my friends thought I was crazy. "Go after the money," they told me. But they only saw the rewards and didn't understand my motivation. When I was sworn in as a City of Meriden police officer, it was one of the greatest days of my life. I had a shiny badge on my chest, the weight of the gun on my side, and exciting challenges ahead. My engine was running, the open road lay before me, and my foot was twitching on the gas pedal like a drop of water in a hot frying pan.

Like every other cop in this world, I could go on forever with "war stories" collected over my 30-plus-year career in law enforcement. Some of them are funny, many of them sad, and others terrifying. Details often come back to you at night in your dreams: the baby who died in your arms as you tried in vain to breathe life into her; a family's only child dying in your arms after being hit head-on by a drunk driver; telling families that a loved one had been killed and holding them tight as they try to beat their hands on your chest in agony; delivering an undocumented immigrant's baby on a dirt floor basement where the parents were hiding; getting black eyes and broken bones trying to break up fights or take people into custody;

being rammed by a fleeing felon at over 100 miles per hour and being cut out of the cruiser by the fire department; the look on your wife's face after she's been driven to the hospital, by another state trooper thinking you died; friends who lost their lives in the line of duty; guns pointed at you and knives pulled on you; fear, panic, laughter, and tears. Every place you look, you see reminders of a career that enriched and drained you to the point of near collapse. It is no wonder that so many cops move away when they retire. It's not always for warmer climates, but rather a fresh canvas to paint the rest of their lives on, without painful memories at every turn.

On July 4, 1988, after being with the Meriden Police Department for two years, I met the woman I fell in love with. My best friend since childhood, Mark, was sitting with me on my parents' porch at our beach house. My sister came walking in with a woman who immediately caught my attention. She was beautiful, with green eyes that wouldn't let you look away and blond hair that shined in the sunlight. My sister introduced Debi to Mark and me, telling us she was from Wisconsin. We exchanged a few pleasant remarks, and they headed out to the beach.

As Debi walked away with my sister, I turned to Mark and said, "That's the girl I'm going to marry."

He just smirked and said, "Yeah, right." I told him that not only was I sure of it, I asked him right there to be my best man, and he just laughed. I knew with every fiber of my body that this was the woman I was meant to be with. The problem was, she hadn't gotten that memo, and the pursuit wouldn't be easy.

I asked my sister for Debi's phone number, and she reluctantly gave it to me. I called Debi about six times and asked her if she would like to go out to dinner or a movie. Every time she politely declined, explaining that she was going to be moving back to Wisconsin soon and didn't want to get involved with anyone. A less determined man would have taken the hint, but I've never been accused of being less determined about anything.

Then I got a call from my sister. Debi's friend had borrowed her car and fell asleep driving home late at night. She rolled the car and thankfully wasn't injured. However, she did receive a ticket for reckless driving, a standard citation back then for falling asleep while driving. The fine could be up to $1,500, but almost never was. My sister asked if I could do anything about the ticket because if her friend had to pay $1,500, she couldn't afford to pay the insurance deductible.

Luckily, the Superior Court for traffic violations in Connecticut was in Meriden, and I knew many of the state attorneys who worked there. I told my sister that I could probably do something to help, but in return, Debi would have to go to dinner with me. My sister put the phone against her chest, and I heard some mumbling, and then sounding slightly aggravated, my sister answered, "Fine!" A smile extended across my face as I told her we could get dinner and a movie that coming Saturday night.

I spoke with one of the prosecutors who simply dropped the charge to "failure to keep right of a solid line," a common dropdown plea on these types of cases. Debi's friend paid the $30 fine and the insurance deductible, and I was going to get to look into those beautiful green eyes over dinner.

Debi would tell you that she should have known what she was getting herself into as we had dinner and I took her to see *Die Hard*, which was just out in the theaters. I guess a real romantic would have looked for something a bit mushier. After the movie, I took her home and shook her hand, telling her I had a great night. No pressure, no moves, just a polite thank-you. I waited a couple of days to call her again, and she reluctantly agreed to go out to dinner again.

Two dates turned into dozens, and we found ourselves together all the time when we weren't working. It just took her a while to come to the same realization I had from the start: We were meant to be together. Three beautiful children and 30 years later, there is still nobody on this earth that I would rather be with, and I'm as much in love now as I was then.

A few months after Debi and I were married, my dad was driving with my mom up to see us in New Hampshire. We had great news we wanted to share with them: Debi was pregnant. It would be a great weekend, as my mom and dad were eager for grandchildren. My sister Kristen and her husband, Eugene, beat us to the "first grandchild" award, but we were in hot pursuit. Our family loved kids.

My dad was one of the first people I knew who had a car phone, and I was surprised when my mother called me on it. There was fear in her voice as she explained that my dad seemed to be lost and was talking about meeting me at a car auction. I asked to speak with him, and he started telling me that he couldn't remember the address of the car auction. The only time my dad and I were supposed to go to an old car auction was when I was 17 years old, but something came up and we never went. I was confused and asked why he was looking for the auction place, and he replied, "We're supposed to go to the auction." My stomach suddenly twisted. I knew there was something terribly wrong, and I asked Dad to put Mom back on the phone.

I explained to my mom that something wasn't right and she needed to get Dad to our house. I talked to my dad again and told him that we would head over to the auction when he got to our house, and he accepted that. I asked him if he remembered how to get to our house. And he replied that he did.

I hung up the phone and looked at Debi, the cold dread climbing up my spine as if I were just pulling up to a fatal accident scene. We waited anxiously until Mom and Dad arrived almost two hours later. My dad came in smiling and happy, while my mother was walking in behind him with her eyes wide and a look of panic on her face. She quietly told me that they had gotten lost several times after speaking with me, but my mother was able to get them back on track.

We took my dad to Concord Hospital and explained what had happened. The emergency room doctor was very nice, and after some tests and X-rays, he told me that I should get my dad back home and arrange for a physician there to evaluate him. He was afraid that my dad had a brain tumor. We were crushed.

I drove my dad back to Connecticut, and Debi followed with my mom. My dad seemed perfectly lucid, and I tried to convince myself that maybe it was not as bad as it sounded. We took him to Bridge-port Hospital, where they gave him a CAT scan. A couple of hours later, I saw the doctor who had examined him walking down the hall, toward us with another doctor. They were laughing and talking, and my heart jumped. He didn't look upset or worried, and I glanced at Debi, hoping for the best. When the doctor came near us, his face suddenly became serious, and he simply said, "Your father has a very malignant brain tumor, and nothing can be done. You should get his affairs in order. He has maybe six months." I just stared at him, unable to comprehend what I had just heard. Debi grabbed my arm, and we sat down.

I looked back up at the doctor and said, "There must be something we can do?" He just shook his head.

We did everything possible to save my dad. When they had him on high doses of steroids, the brain pressure would reduce, and he was lucid and knew what was going on. It was during those times that we had some of the most heartfelt talks of my life. I asked him if he was scared knowing that the prognosis was not good, and he said very matter-of-factly, "No, not at all."

I was surprised and said, "I wish I could be that brave."

He just looked at me somewhat surprised and said, "I know that God has a plan. And I know that you will take care of your mom and the girls when I leave." At the most critical point a person could think of, facing mortality, my dad was comfortable with his faith, and he had confidence in me to carry on. I didn't realize it at that moment, but he was passing the torch.

Debi, now a few months pregnant, began traveling back and forth to Connecticut to take my dad to Sloan Kettering Hospital in New York, where they had a world-famous reputation for treating cancer patients. She, my sister Kristen, and my brother-in-law Eugene would take turns navigating the traffic nightmares of driving into New York City every other day to take my father for treatments until the time came that he had to be admitted.

I had been working midnight shifts as a state trooper and had only gotten to bed that morning about two hours before the phone rang. I don't even remember who it was that called, but the message was clear: "Your father has slipped into a semi-comatose state, and your wife is in early labor. She may lose the baby. You should get back to Connecticut." My brother-in-law Shane was staying with us in New Hampshire at that time, and he drove me to Connecticut. I was numb. When I arrived, Debi had been stabilized and would be released later that day. Finally, some good news! I stopped and said a heartfelt thank-you to God.

From there, I went to Sloan Kettering to see my dad. When I arrived, I was met by my aunt and my mom, both of whom were crying in the hall. As I walked into my dad's room, I looked at him lying on the bed, a white blanket covering him up to his neck. He was breathing, but his eyes were closed, and the nurse warned me that he wouldn't be able to open his eyes or speak with the medication. It was a gut punch when I realized at that moment that I would never hear his voice again. I took hold of his hand and bent down to whisper into his ear, "Dad, if you can hear me, squeeze my hand." He squeezed my hand. I told him to squeeze my hand once for yes and twice for no, and I asked him if he understood. He squeezed once. I then asked him if he was in any pain, and he squeezed twice. "Thank God," I thought to myself.

There was nothing that I could say to him at that time that we hadn't already discussed. I leaned in and whispered in his ear, "Dad, I think that you are getting ready to go and see Grandma and Grandpa," and he squeezed my hand once. Then I said, "You know how much I love you, and we will be together again very soon." He just squeezed my hand and kept squeezing. I started to cry, having fought so hard to hold it together. He then squeezed my hand twice, as if to tell me not to cry. I leaned across his body, hugging him hard, sobbing. I took hold of his hand once more, leaned down to kiss his forehead, and he squeezed hard once again, and then he released my hand. He had let me go.

Looking down at him, I knew that I would never see him again.

He had been the backbone of a family that had seen its fair share of tragedies. My sister Linda was 21 years old and engaged to be married when she and her best friend were killed in a car accident in 1984 after a tractor-trailer jumped the median and hit her head-on. My sister Debbie would fight a life-long battle with addiction to prescription drugs that tortured my parents through a stream of rehabilitation attempts. She would never be able to overcome those demons that took her too young after my parents had passed.

My mom was diagnosed with lung cancer about 10 years after my dad had passed. She would survive until 2005, after going through multiple rounds of chemo treatments and being tethered to an oxygen line for the last year. I was in Florida when I received a late evening phone call from my sister Kristen, saying that Mom was on the way to the hospital with chest pain and difficulty breathing. She told me I should get to Connecticut as quickly as possible, and I was on the earliest flight I could get out the next morning.

I called Debi, and she immediately put the kids in our Suburban that night and with hastily packed bags started a mad dash halfway across the country. She drove 18 hours straight through and would get to Connecticut only a few hours after me. My wife is incredible.

My brother-in-law picked me up at the airport and rushed me to the hospital, as my mom had deteriorated further while I was traveling. We were only a few miles from the hospital when my sister called crying. My mom had passed, sitting up in bed, when she suffered a massive heart attack.

When I reached the hospital, she was still sitting up in bed with her head tipped gently to the side. My sister was sitting in the corner crying quietly. I hugged her and then walked over to my mom, putting my arms around her and placing my hand on her head. She was still warm, and I leaned down to her ear and said, "Mom, I know you can hear me. Don't worry about us. We will be fine. Tell Dad we send our love, and we will all be together soon." Tears started flowing, and I just held her. It is a sobering moment when you realize the people who brought you into this life are now both gone.

In the days, weeks, and months to come, my wife carried me through as I poured myself back into my work. As our children were growing up, they saw their father in many different lights. When they were very young, they saw the uniformed New Hampshire state trooper: clean-cut, squared away, determined, compassionate, and eager to serve the public.

While I was in uniform, I was recognized each of my first five years for apprehending the highest number of DWI operators. It wasn't because I had anything against drinking, but because I saw DWI as one of the biggest threats on the road to the innocent. You only have to hold a dying 16-year-old boy in your arms once, after he was struck head-on by a drunk driver, to understand the passion that drove me.

Although I pursued DWIs aggressively, my lieutenant called me in one day to ask why I gave out so few tickets and so many warnings. I was honest and just said, "I'm not a hypocrite." He cocked his head, waiting for the rest of the explanation, and I told him that I drove over the speed limit often, as did he. I sometimes forgot to signal for a turn, drove through a yellow light, and committed other mundane traffic violations. It was my belief that when I turned on those red and blue lights, 90 percent of my job was done. I knew that sinking feeling when you looked in the rearview mirror to see those lights and suddenly realized you were doing something wrong. If I walked up to speak with you and you were honest, respectful, and contrite, you likely weren't getting a ticket. I was a bit more Andy Griffith in my approach to law enforcement. The lieutenant listened carefully, nodded, and told me he understood. No lecture, no demands for more tickets; he just wanted to know why. He trusted my judgment.

After five years as a uniformed state trooper, I was promoted to detective and went into undercover narcotics, where the short hair became long, the clean-shaven face grew a beard, and my grubby dress was appropriate for my assignment. It took time for my family to adjust, including my wife, who was always the consummate neat freak. I remember telling her that she shouldn't iron my Harley T-shirts anymore because it was difficult explaining the military creases to the crack dealers.

The move from pursuing criminals as a uniformed trooper to dealing with criminals as an undercover cop was challenging. The ideals were the same, but the approach was completely different. You had to assume a new look, a new identity, and a willingness to strip away the protective armor provided by your uniform and bulletproof vest to appear seedy and shifty like the people you were dealing with.

On top of all this, your close-up encounters with the bad guys were usually alone, with a cover team listening intently for your trouble code word over the body wire, transmitting the conversations at a distance that more than likely couldn't help you if things went bad. Your best weapon was not the gun on your hip but the opening between your nose and chin.

I remember coming home from work one day and my wife had a perturbed look on her face. I asked what the problem was, and she explained that she had to go into school that day and have a quiet conversation with the teacher of our older daughter, Caitlin, about my law enforcement career and present undercover assignment. Apparently, when the teacher was asked what each of the children's daddies did, Caitlin said, "My daddy used to be a state trooper, but now he does drugs." Oh boy. That prompted a call from the school pretty quickly.

The kids were too young to understand what their dad was doing in undercover work, but they knew I was still one of the good guys. They would sit on my lap and rub my beard or laugh as I nuzzled it on their necks to tickle them. I remember being glad that they didn't understand what I did because I didn't want them scared by the danger that my wife understood all too well. I was just their dad with long hair and a beard.

While working undercover in New Hampshire, I attended a thermal image school for law enforcement in Lake Tahoe. At that conference, I met a special agent from the Wisconsin Department of Justice (DOJ), Division of Narcotics Enforcement. We talked for hours, and what surprised me was that he had over 20 years on the job and still had positive things to say about his agency. Most cops with several years under their belt can pick their agency apart like maggots on a carcass, but he didn't.

Knowing that my wife was from Wisconsin, he encouraged me to apply for a special agent position. I was reluctant to think about it because I truly loved my job as a state trooper. It was everything I had ever wanted, and the thought of leaving it made my heart sink. I spoke with my wife about it, and she couldn't hide her enthusiasm for the prospect. She had wanted to move home to Wisconsin for years, and this certainly looked like the opportunity to do it.

I flew to Wisconsin when they offered the next special agent civil service exam. I sat in a large auditorium and took the test along with many others testing for a variety of state positions. The largest part of the exam consisted of being given a group of photos and having 10 minutes to study them. No notes, just observation and then a lot of questions on those pictures. I was a cop, so I carefully looked at the descriptions of the people, the vehicles, the backgrounds, the colors, the clothes. All the stuff a good cop would do instinctively.

Unfortunately, the test was not made by a cop. The questions instead focused on the number of ketchup bottles, how many tables in the restaurant, what was the color of the tablecloths, how many tables had salt shakers? Needless to say, my first outing was less than inspiring when my ranking came out. There would be no job that year, but that was fine with me because I loved being a state trooper and got the Brownie points with my wife for trying.

The next year, I again flew to Wisconsin to take the very same exam with the very same pictures. But I got a better result because I remembered how useless it was from a cop's perspective and remembered more of what they wanted. When I completed the exam, I immediately went to the car and wrote down all the questions I could remember. In all, I recalled 80 out of the 100 questions. But, alas, it was not good enough to make the short list. Yet another year passed, and Wisconsin remained a long distance away.

Over the next year, I studied those questions to the point of having them memorized. This time when I went back to take the same exam, the work paid off. I scored very high on the list. The test was for the position of special agent with the Division of Narcotics Enforcement and its sister agency, the Division of Criminal Investigation (DCI). In September 1989, I received a call from the special agent I had met in Lake Tahoe, and he said I was going to be offered the position by both divisions. He wanted to know what the Division of Narcotics Enforcement could do to sweeten their offer, and I told him that an appointment in Madison would be the best for us since that is where my wife's family was. Minutes later, I received a phone call from the special agent in charge of training at the Division of Narcotics Enforcement and was offered the position of special agent in the Madison regional office.

With my wife staring at me as I answered the phone, I was torn between being happy to please my wife and devastated to walk away from the job I loved. "Happy wife, happy life" ran through my mind as I accepted the appointment, which would start on October 11, 1999. When I hung up the phone, she screamed with joy and wrapped her arms around my neck. We packed up our family, sold our house, and moved to Wisconsin. I took a $20,000 pay cut, and we knew we would have to tighten our belts to make things work, but my wife was ecstatic, and the rest would work out. She always made things work out.

After receiving the word that I was going to Wisconsin, I notified my lieutenant, and he notified the captain. Word traveled quickly, and when my letter of resignation got to the captain, he called me and said, "I'm not accepting your resignation. Instead, I am going to put you on a year's leave of absence just in case you want to come back. We don't want to lose you, Ed, and you will always be welcome back here."

My eyes teared up as he spoke, and I knew in my heart I was leaving something I loved. "Happy wife, happy life. Happy wife, happy life." I kept saying it to myself and knew that the love for my wife outweighed what any job could offer me. I quietly closed the door on my path back to the Granite State and looked toward Wisconsin. ❧

FORWARD TO WISCONSIN

In October 1999, Attorney General Jim Doyle swore in a group of new special agents, including me. Fortunately, our house in New Hampshire sold quickly, and we had money to live on because the pay with the Wisconsin DOJ was so low. My sainted in-laws had a rental property in Madison that they were refurbishing, and we lived there while the construction was going on. Not ideal, but we had a roof over our heads and family nearby.

Our younger daughter, Emily, had been diagnosed in New Hampshire with hydrocephalus at 18 months old and had to undergo brain shunt surgery to survive, so our insurance was more important than anything. When she was four years old, Dr. Joe Phillips was the chief of pediatric neurosurgery at Dartmouth-Hitchcock Medical Center and diagnosed her with a Chiari malformation of the skull, which was crimping her spinal cord. Emily required dangerous surgery that involved cutting part of her skull away from her brain stem and spine. Dr. Phillips saved our daughter's life, and we are eternally grateful to the finest doctor we have ever met.

Over the course of her life, Emily has undergone over a dozen surgical procedures related to her hydrocephalus, and we simply could not take the chance of being uninsured. I took the COBRA option on my insurance with the New Hampshire State Police since Wisconsin did not give insurance until you had been on the job for a certain time period back then. We'll never forget when my first paycheck came and we saw that it had a small dollar amount in parentheses. I asked the administrative assistant at DOJ headquarters what that meant, and she explained that I actually owed the state that much after they paid my COBRA. It was a bit concerning, but I was confident that God had a plan, and with our family behind us we would persevere.

I took on my role with the Division of Narcotics Enforcement with my usual gusto. I gave it my all, made myself available to anyone who needed help, and focused on making a difference. Early on in my DOJ career, I watched as the Division of Criminal Investigation became embroiled in the Wisconsin caucus scandal, which would result in the leading legislators from both parties getting convicted on charges related to corruption in office. It became obvious that working for the attorney general in the DOJ would bring me closer to politics than I had ever been before, but my concern was for law enforcement, and I needed to stay focused.

As the caucus scandal plodded on, I watched with dismay as politicians scrambled to cover up their actions, pointed fingers, blamed each other, and did exactly what politicians were known to do—cover their own backsides. Even the political affiliations of DCI investigators assigned to the case were raised by some of those under investigation, so I resolved then and there that I would not vote while in my position working for a politician. Not that I didn't cherish my right to vote, but I didn't want anyone ever intimating that my integrity and objectiveness were questionable because of who I may have voted for or given money to. I wanted to be above that fray and sacrificed my rights to maintain my neutrality.

Subsequently, Jim Doyle was elected governor, and we found ourselves with a new attorney general named Peg Lautenschlager. I had known Peg when she was the U.S. attorney for the Western District of Wisconsin and found her to be friendly, approachable, and reasonable. I will never forget the first time I met Peg. I was in a federal trial on one of my drug cases, and court was recessed while the jury retired to deliberate. The assistant U.S. attorney prosecuting the case and I went to a nearby restaurant to wait. When we walked in, I saw Peg, Deputy U.S. Attorney Dan Bach, and a couple of other attorneys. We went over, and I was introduced to Peg for the first time. We talked for a few moments before I interrupted her and said, "Peg, these stuffed suits haven't told you, but I will: You have some spinach in your teeth," and I pointed at my teeth to where her leafy distraction sat. She stopped, took her finger, and removed the spinach. Then she turned to Dan and punched him in the arm exclaiming, "Why didn't you tell me that?" We all broke into laughter, and I told her that if nothing else, I would always be honest with her.

After Peg was elected attorney general, she coordinated a merger of the Division of Criminal Investigation and the Division of Narcotics Enforcement. I thought it was a good move and would broaden the resources while eliminating the duplication of having two criminal investigative agencies in one department. We all became DCI agents.

At that time, the DCI special agents were represented by the Wisconsin Professional Employees Council (WPEC) as our union. I had never been a big union supporter, but I maintained my membership in all my law enforcement positions. Although I disagreed with some of the tactics used by unions, I did see the benefit that they provided in contract negotiations and in dealing with heavy-handed supervisors who abused their authority. The unions had long ago established their political power and would obviously have a better opportunity to advocate on our behalf than we would alone.

The DCI agents were represented at WPEC by one of our agents on the bargaining support committee. She grew tired of the union issues and announced she would be leaving her position as representative for the agents. There was a flurry of activity as the agents discussed who would replace her. It needed to be someone in Madison since that is where the activities all happened, but nobody wanted to take it on. Finally, I said I would do it and reluctantly went to the WPEC bargaining support committee.

There, I met Art Foeste, the WPEC president, and we hit it off. I found him to be very practical, and he understood the challenges that we faced as state law enforcement officers. Assigned to the bargaining support committee, I soon found out why the position was so frustrating. The support committee was charged with sorting through the myriad of proposals from members for inclusion in the contract negotiations. Some of those proposals were absolutely ridiculous, such as an extra 30 minutes added to the lunch period for employees with over 20 years on the job so they would have time to take a nap. Another one that caught my attention was a request that same-sex couples be given a stipend of $7,000 to undergo in vitro fertilization.

One of my well-known traits, for better or worse, is being unafraid to speak up on issues that I feel are wrong. I pointed out that taxpayers would not be sympathetic to the proposal of older employees taking a nap while working or same-sex couples getting a monetary benefit that was not available to other couples. This made me somewhat divisive to far-left members of the committee, but it caught Art Foeste's attention. He called me a few weeks later and asked if I would join the WPEC Executive Council. I cautioned him that my "common sense" might offend some of his most vocal, left-leaning members, and he insisted that was why he wanted me. I wasn't afraid to say what many others were thinking. I was to become the lone conservative voice, which is not the most comfortable place in any union.

Subsequently, I was appointed to the bargaining committee and named as co-chair. This was my first real peek under the hood at how unions, politicians, and government agencies coexisted. Demands, counter-demands, quiet conversations, sidebars, unwritten agreements, favors, political action committees, pledged support, and threats of withdrawing support were all part of the constant hum of the machine that comprised unions and politicians of both parties.

One of the issues that arose and troubled me during my time on the WPEC Executive Council, was the creation of a Political Action Committee (PAC). At that time, Cory Mason was not in an elected position but was consulting with WPEC on political issues. It was Cory who urged the creation of the PAC and would be instrumental in guiding its creation.

Fundamentally, I disagreed with the PAC philosophy and the manner in which it was to be instituted. Initially, the plan was to simply allocate a portion of membership dues to the PAC, which would then be distributed to politicians who favored union positions. I objected to this because I knew there were people like me who were conservative-minded and did not want their union dues going to politicians.

It was clearly understood that those PAC donations would be going to Democratic legislators, and my feeling was this was blatantly partisan. There could obviously be a backlash effect if Republicans took control of the legislature and wanted to settle scores for the union money being dumped into the races. That fear would manifest itself years later.

What bothered me most was this PAC creation was going to be somewhat obscured from members by just allocating a portion of their dues without their agreement. Subsequently, I pushed for letting the members decide if they wanted to contribute to the PAC rather than just having their dues committed to a political cause they may not have agreed with. Ultimately, the decision was to allow the members to decide if they wished to make contributions to the PAC. It was not a popular decision with some, but it was the right thing to do.

The DCI administrator at the time, Jim Warren, was well liked and respected across the division. A retired Milwaukee police inspector, Jim knew what it was like to lead people and take care of his staff. He had a saying that I adopted as my credo: "We Exist to Assist." That simple phrase captured my career aspirations in four words. Jim was very direct, and we hit it off well. He knew that I was involved in the union on the Executive Council, and we met to discuss the union grievances that were outstanding at the time of the merger of the two divisions.

Jim quickly resolved all those issues and made it clear to me that he didn't want union problems distracting from our responsibilities. He suggested that before anyone filed grievances going forward, we would speak first to try and resolve the issues. It was his willingness to be reasonable and our ability to speak frankly that resulted in no grievances being filed from that point forward while I represented the agents. Reasonable people can disagree, but they can also compromise, and that we did.

After the merger, I was approached by Craig Klyve, director of the Investigative Services Bureau, and asked if I would be interested in transferring from the Narcotics Bureau to the Investigative Services Bureau, Technical Services Unit (Covert Surveillance). Craig was one of the most affable people in the DCI and was well liked by everyone. He was always willing to help people, at work or in their personal lives, and he was a man of integrity. He put in long hours and always looked out for his staff, which was one of the things that I admired about him.

My affinity for technology and constant pursuit of better equipment for our work was known to all by that time. Plus, there was a lot of overtime available in the unit, and the extra money would be helpful. I interviewed for the position and got it.

I'll never forget going to my supervisor at the time and telling him that I would be transferring to the Technical Services Unit. He wasn't happy, and I took that as a veiled compliment that he appreciated what I did for the regional field office. He looked me in the eye and said, "You're going to be nothing but a VCR repairman for the rest of your career," and then walked out of my office. Several years later, after I was named the administrator of the DCI and he had retired, I was in a Gander Mountain store shopping. Suddenly, behind me, I heard his unmistakable voice say, "Ed, word on the street is you are the new DCI administrator."

I turned to find him standing there and replied with a big smile, "Well, that can't possibly be true. You told me I would be a VCR repairman the rest of my life." We both got a good laugh out of that and then spent a few minutes catching up.

I have always regretted leaving college in my senior year to become a cop. While I had intended to go back and finish my education, life happened. I met the love of my life, we had three beautiful kids, and there were bills to pay. The years slid by, and before I knew it, my kids were teenagers, and I was in my mid-forties.

My wife and I preached to our kids about how important college was and that they needed to get their degrees. Then one day my oldest daughter said to me at dinner, "Dad, if college is so important, why didn't you finish?" It was a cold slap in the face of fatherhood and a bracing reminder to practice what you preach.

I looked at my daughter for a few moments and replied, "You're right, I need to go back and finish my degree as an example for you and to do what I said I would do 20 years ago."

I enrolled in classes at Madison College and the University of Wisconsin in Madison. It took about 18 months, working full-time as a special agent and going to school at night and on weekends to get it completed, but I finally received my bachelor's degree in business administration. Then I had a new lesson for them: Don't wait until you're in your forties to go to college. It was difficult, especially if you worked at the tempo and intensity that I did.

As a special agent, I took on the role of pursuing new technology through various federal grant programs. There was no agency funding to purchase much-needed equipment, and there was never a line of people asking to get involved in grant applications, narrative writing, and cost analysis. So, I did it myself with Director Craig Klyve's blessing. One of the federal programs I began working with was the Counterdrug Technology Assessment Center in the Office of National Drug Control Policy. They offered exceptional law enforcement equipment through a federal program, and I began applying.

We were fortunate enough to get awarded several pieces of equipment, like thermal imagers, body wires, and covert cameras. It was a great program to work with, and I began giving them unsolicited feedback on their equipment along with success stories of how it was used in Wisconsin.

Fond of my efforts, the Counterdrug Technology Assessment Center reached out to me on several occasions about reviewing equipment they were considering for placement in their program. Eventually, the DCI became a test bed for new counterdrug technologies, and Wisconsin started receiving the newest stuff available. One thing led to another, and I ended up on their technical review committee, which benefited Wisconsin as we were awarded millions of dollars in technologies that would play key roles in some of the largest criminal cases the state has ever seen.

Around this same time, while I was in Washington, D.C., for technology meetings, I received a call from Administrator Jim Warren. He asked me what I knew about fusion centers, and I replied, "Nothing." I was a cop, not a nuclear physicist.

He said, "Good. Starting Monday, you're running one; it's an intelligence fusion center." I asked what that was and where it was located. He simply said, "That's the hitch; you have to build it from scratch. Come see me Friday when you get back, and I'll explain."

When I flew back on Friday, Jim handed me a CD-ROM from the Bureau of Justice Assistance in Washington that detailed what the Intelligence Fusion Center vision was and how such a center should be implemented. He told me this was coming straight from the governor's office, and I had a million dollars to get it built, equipped, and operational. Pretty heady stuff for a lowly special agent, but I didn't balk. I took that CD-ROM home and spent the weekend absorbing the information it contained.

The next Monday, I came in with a rough sketch of the process we needed to follow in identifying space, meeting national security clearance requirements, hiring, construction, equipment, partner agencies, and so forth. To accomplish this, Jim named me acting special agent in charge so that I would have supervisory authority to pull the operation together. In nine months, the Wisconsin Statewide Information Center was opened as the state's Intelligence Fusion Center. Partnering with the FBI and Department of Homeland Security, the Wisconsin Statewide Information Center took on its new role in sharing critical law enforcement information across the state and country, while also supporting criminal investigations and counterterrorism work. Eventually, I was asked to work with the Milwaukee Police Department in starting up its own intelligence fusion center.

My work with the Wisconsin Statewide Information Center and with other fusion centers nationwide led to some notoriety as we worked diligently to further this noble information-sharing cause. After the 9/11 attacks, it became all too clear that stovepipes in law enforcement information sharing contributed to the terror that wrenched the guts of our country and changed our lives forever. Subsequently, I was elected the first president of the National Fusion Center Association, which represented all the state fusion center directors across the country. It wasn't because of any great skill on my part, but simply because I did what needed to be done and got the ball rolling.

One tool that I used for criminal investigations with great success in New Hampshire was the court-ordered wiretap. However, Wisconsin rarely used wiretaps, and the last one had been done years before I arrived. With the advent of digital communications and improved intercept capabilities, I broached the subject with Administrator Jim Warren. He approved the plan to acquire one of the new wiretap systems for the state, and we were fortunate to receive a $500,000 system as a test bed for the new technology. From nearly zero wiretaps to dozens, Wisconsin made the leap to prominence in telecommunication intercepts and brought that ability to the forefront in law enforcement. Newspapers commented on the sudden use of wiretaps and the explosion of defendants suddenly being brought before judges on charges coming from those intercepts. From large-scale narcotics investigations to cold-case homicides and counterterrorism, Wisconsin DCI was making a difference.

As this was all going on, I was asked to apply for the permanent special agent in charge position in the Investigative Services Bureau, working for Director Klyve. I was reluctant to apply because I enjoyed being in the field and engaging with the law enforcement agencies we supported across the state. However, I was assured that I would still have opportunities to get in the field, and so I was convinced to throw my name in the hat. Subsequently, I was promoted to that position and took on the responsibilities it entailed.

During this time, the country was still reeling from the effects of the 9/11 attacks and the paradigm shift that occurred in homeland security. Because of his position as DCI administrator, Jim Warren sat on the Governor's Homeland Security Council. Often his schedule would conflict with the Homeland Security Council meetings, so he asked me to serve as his alternate based on my involvement with the fusion center, wiretapping, and counterterrorism. By virtue of my position on the council and running the fusion center, I was required to obtain and maintain a Tier 3 Secret level national security clearance.

Overall, the DCI relationship with Attorney General Peg Lautenschlager was a very good one. However, there was a bump in the road near the end of her term when her administration had wanted to investigate Governor Jim Doyle with regard to some state property transactions. She and Doyle were not getting along, and it appeared that the desire to investigate Doyle might be politically based. When they went to Jim Warren to request the investigation, Jim refused based on the lack of a criminal element. That aggravated Peg's team but clearly demonstrated the value of having a neutral and detached DCI administrator who would not misuse the agency. It also demonstrated the importance of the historical precedence that the DCI administrator is above politics and not subject to replacement at will by the attorney general. That premise would be shredded in the next two Republican administrations.

In the next election, Peg lost to Republican J.B. Van Hollen, who was the U.S. attorney in the Western District of Wisconsin. I was sorry to see Peg go, as she was good to the DCI and let us do our job. When Van Hollen came into office, there was some apprehension since Peg was so well liked. Van Hollen was an unknown, but his immediate focus on tightening up things like dress codes and hours of work seemed like a conservative Republican mantra after 12 years of Democrats leading the DOJ.

Jim Warren and Van Hollen began to bang heads early on about how the division should be run. Historically, and by law, the DCI administrator position was a civil service position that had to be earned through the civil service selection process. It was not an appointed position to the unclassified service as most administrator positions were in state government. That was by design; the legislature obviously understood the importance of the DCI administrator being above politics since it could be tasked with conducting criminal investigations of politicians. If the DCI administrator could just be removed at the whim of the attorney general, then that obviously compromised the objectivity of the position and made it nothing more than another political appointment that could be strong-armed by the attorney general. That would be a dangerous overreach and abuse of authority if the DCI was used in that manner.

Van Hollen's team took the position that it ran the DCI, and the DCI would be doing what he told it to do. Now, there has always been a fine line for the DCI administrator between doing the work of the DCI and simultaneously supporting the attorney general's initiatives. But, that fine line was all but erased by Van Hollen and his staff, who made it clear they felt the DCI administrator position was under their control. Administrator Jim Warren became increasingly agitated with the way the Van Hollen administration was trying to control the division, and it showed.

All of the attorneys general before Van Hollen understood the necessity of a neutral and detached civil service DCI administrator position, and they honored it. Van Hollen, however, looked at it differently. When he and Warren started disagreeing, Van Hollen made the unprecedented move of trying to force Jim into a civilian position in the Training and Standards Bureau, ending his law enforcement career and changing his retirement benefits without just cause or due process. It was a gross abuse of his authority and placed the DCI in a precarious position.

Jim decided that putting up with this obvious violation of law and historical precedent wasn't worth the time or headaches, and he retired. I always wished Jim had fought that move for the good of the agency and the stability of the position, but alas, he did not, and the future of the DCI administrator position hung in the balance.

After Jim left, I was contacted by the DOJ administrator of Management Services and asked if I would be interested in serving as acting administrator while a civil service process was conducted to replace Jim. I was surprised by that offer because I was not close to Van Hollen or any politician. Instead of jumping at it, I offered my considered advice to Van Hollen's staff. I pointed out to them that I was only a special agent in charge, and there were four directors between me and the administrator position. To keep the troops calm, in what was quickly being perceived as a Van Hollen coup over the DCI, I suggested they appoint an existing director to the position instead of me. Ultimately, that advice was taken, and they appointed Mike Myszewski as acting administrator and subsequently as permanent DCI administrator.

Mike was a nice enough guy, but he struggled with the leadership role that DCI required. As DCI administrator, you were expected to be the law enforcement face of the agency across the state and out with your peers building partnerships. Mike was a bit more introverted and tended to stay at headquarters, where he was perceived as a servant of the attorney general who had forced out the much-admired Jim Warren. Jim was the consummate goodwill ambassador with law enforcement statewide; Mike tended to stay near the flagpole. Tensions in the DCI began to build, and staff were becoming very dissatisfied with Mike's level of engagement with them and our law enforcement peers. Several of the staff took the unusual step of expressing their discontent to high-level DOJ officials and eventually to the attorney general himself.

In 2009, I'd been serving as Investigative Services special agent in charge for about four years when the administrator of Wisconsin Emergency Management announced his retirement. The Wisconsin Statewide Information Center worked closely with the Department of Military Affairs by virtue of our classified briefings, counterterrorism work, and responses to manmade and natural disasters. I had become close with previous Adjutant General Al Wilkening and current Adjutant General Don Dunbar through the course of those duties. Subsequently, General Dunbar asked me if I would be interested in him referring my name for the governor's appointment as administrator of Wisconsin Emergency Management. I was flattered but explained that I couldn't take a political appointment because of the career risk. Don said that he wanted to have the governor's legal chief call me to explain the facts behind a gubernatorial appointment when serving in the unclassified service before I made a decision.

I received a call from Susan Crawford, legal chief for Governor Jim Doyle, and she explained that by taking a gubernatorial appointment from a classified position, I would be guaranteed by law to return to my position as special agent in charge in the Investigative Services Bureau. In fact, she advised that the law said that I would return to my same position and position number. After considering that information and the impact the higher salary would have on my retirement to benefit my family, I agreed to meet with the governor. After meeting with Governor Doyle, I was offered the position of administrator of Wisconsin Emergency Management and accepted. This was a difficult decision because it meant that, at least for some period of time, I wouldn't be doing law enforcement work. I'd have no badge and no gun for the first time in over 20 years. Most people would not understand the hesitation that decision would involve, but to a cop, it was akin to walking naked down the middle of Main Street.

I went to Mike Myszewski and let him know that I had been

offered the gubernatorial appointment as Wisconsin Emergency Management administrator, and he was not very happy. Mike knew that I had my hands in so many DCI baskets and served in many key roles that it would be tough to replace me in the short term. He told me that if I left and tried to come back, he would "send my ass to Superior" to work in the far northern field office. I just kept my mouth shut and let Mike vent because I knew what the governor's legal chief had told me, and it didn't match Mike's emotional response.

When I left, I was admittedly reluctant because the DCI was my home. It was the agency and the job I had committed to and moved my family across country to work for. Mike's style of leadership was part of the reason I chose to take the appointment, but that was not something I wanted to share with him. There was no use burning a bridge that I might have to cross again someday.

I started my position with Wisconsin Emergency Management just a few days later, in June 2009. After going through the usual paperwork for a gubernatorial appointment and changing agencies, I then went through my confirmation hearings and was confirmed by the Senate in a unanimous vote. One of the Republicans on the committee that ran my confirmation hearing said at the end on the record "There are a lot of things this governor does that we don't understand, but this time it looks like he finally got it right."

Life changed dramatically from that day on. I went from being a self-sufficient division supervisor to a state agency head in the blink of an eye. Although it was a daunting move, the Department of Military Affairs made it as painless as possible. This was an agency that knew how to pivot on a dime, make a decision, and move forward. The military and civilian staff were some of the best people I ever met in my career, and the way they did things was consistent with my personal beliefs: professional, crisp, moving with purpose, and having a shared mission mentality.

Being the administrator of Wisconsin Emergency Management was probably one of the best jobs I ever had. Not because it was a gubernatorial appointment, which many people would be infatuated with, but because of the breadth of the mission: safeguarding people and infrastructure from the worst that man or nature could throw at us. It spoke to my deepest desires to serve a greater good, and I dove in head first. Floods, snowstorms, chemical spills, counterterrorism, disaster response, full-scale and tabletop exercising: It was all so vitally important, and I loved it. If that had been a permanent civil service position, which I think it should be, I would have never left. The position is so critical to the state's ability to respond when things are at their worst, yet there is a revolving door of political appointees who may or may not have enough time to master the skills and challenges the state needs to rely on. Emergency management for the most part was, and should always be, above politics. However, I quickly realized that as the administrator, I would be managing many millions of dollars in grants and disaster relief, which the governor's office always wanted control over. Like so many other things, it was about the money and not the job.

As the governor's appointed agency head, I had responsibilities to him, but most of the time I worked with and for the adjutant general. My division was in his department, and I never was confused about that structure, as some had been in the past. General Dunbar was the best person I ever worked for, and he taught me more about leadership in nine months than I learned in the rest of my professional experience combined. The funny thing about learning how to lead is that often supervisors teach you how *not* to lead. That wasn't the case with Don, and the lessons he taught me became indelible.

The work at Wisconsin Emergency Management was always fast-paced, and during my short tenure, we had several large-scale responses and a presidential disaster declaration to deal with. Unfortunately, when I came into office, we also had some internal strife that had been brought to my attention by staff members who felt that management did not support them prior to my arrival. There was fear of reprisals, unfair handling of personnel issues, and general discontent that permeated throughout our small agency. While many would just ignore the grumbling of staff as insignificant, I saw it as a festering wound that needed attention. When I was made aware of problems, I took them head-on, intent on resolving issues before they became worse.

In speaking with General Dunbar and General Scott Legwold, two of my most trusted advisors and peer supporters, I decided to conduct a Strengths, Weaknesses, Opportunities, and Threats (SWOT) analysis. This internal assessment lets the agency do some introspection and come up with methods of addressing and improving operations and relationships. Ultimately, the exercise did wonders for morale and opened lines of communication that never existed before. My open-door policy was more than just talk, and staff knew they could come speak with me on any issue without fear of retribution. That exercise, and the ensuing changes I brought to the management philosophy, helped us work better as a team.

While busy with my new job, I was distracted by the fact that Mike Myszewski at DCI was refusing to fill my special agent in charge position. After being informed about my restoration rights, he didn't want to promote anyone with the possibility of me being able to come back, and bump them. Unfortunately, this left my former boss and dear friend, Craig Klyve, trying to do his work and mine. He had no frontline supervisor to work directly with staff and no experienced person to write all the grants that I had assumed responsibility for over the years.

Out of concern for Craig, I ended up ghostwriting as much of the various federal grants for him that I could on my own time, but he was still overwhelmed. He called me at home on Sunday evening, October 18, 2009, at about 11:00 p.m. with questions on a grant application he was trying to get submitted by the deadline the next morning. We walked through the application, and I told him he needed to get some help. He was beyond stressed; he was manic. He feared the repercussions of losing a grant that the department had become reliant on. When I hung up the phone, I was very concerned for Craig's well-being. I had never heard him like this before, and I felt he was near the breaking point. Craig's instinct was to dig in and do the work, no matter when or where it needed to be done, even if that meant it would adversely affect him.

I called him on Monday morning, and he had gotten the grant submitted but feared it might not be good enough. I told him that I was going to contact Myszewski and ask him to please fill my position because Craig just couldn't do both of our jobs. He asked me not to, because he didn't want to draw attention to his struggles. That was how Craig was; he suffered in silence but would give the shirt off his back to anyone.

The attorney general was holding his yearly conference that week in the Wisconsin Dells, and I decided that I would go up to the Dells to speak with the deputy attorney general personally. I asked my assistant to quietly clear my schedule, and I went up to meet with Deputy Attorney General Ray Taffora and the DOJ Division of Management Services administrator. I told them about my interactions with Craig, and that I feared he was near the breaking point trying to do both of our jobs. I further told them that Myszewski had been holding the position open because of my restoration rights, but I would happily demote upon restoration to a special agent position if they filled my supervisor position, because Craig needed the help. Letting go of my supervisor's rank and pay was well worth the sacrifice to help a friend.

Two days later, on October 23, 2009, I received a call that Craig had taken his own life. Using his service weapon, he shot himself in his state-issued car, which was parked in his parking spot at the DOJ Risser Justice Center. He was found by his wife, who was also a DOJ attorney, when she went to the Risser building looking for him when he didn't come home. That loss affected me and many others from that day forward. I was overwhelmed with guilt and was convinced that if I had only turned down the Wisconsin Emergency Management position, I would have been there to do the work and Craig would still be with us. My thoughts about improving my retirement and more time with my family had cost the life of a dear friend.

It took many nights of talks with my wife, friends, and ultimately a doctor to come to realize that we can't always take responsibility for the actions of others. We will never know all the demons that Craig wrestled with, but I remain convinced that if I had two minutes to talk with him, I could have changed his mind. How could things get so bad that taking your own life could seem like a reasonable solution? That is the gut-wrenching question that survivors are left with, along with feelings of anger and guilt. They all rush through the mind, and the answers never come. "If only I had two minutes to talk with him" kept ringing in my head. It haunted me then and still does today. Ultimately, it would mean more to me than I could ever imagine.

I was asked to deliver the eulogy at Craig's funeral, and it was an agonizing effort. Nothing makes us question our faith in God like the tragic and senseless death or suffering of others. Conversely, our faith is what we cling to in explaining that God had a plan we are not privy to. So many times throughout my life, this dichotomy has brought me to tears as I tried to reconcile them. It is a struggle that will never end until that time when I make the journey myself and arrive on the other side, only then to find understanding.

In that eulogy, I acknowledged that we would never be able to answer the long list of questions we shared about why Craig decided to leave us. However, I did direct some of my remarks to the DOJ executive staff, including the attorney general, who was in attendance. I encouraged people in leadership to be more responsive to the needs of those who served them. I pointed out that sometimes people who need help the most will say the least in their efforts to please their supervisors or peers. I concluded by stating that it was their responsibility as leaders to expend every possible effort to get their employees the help they needed, and if they couldn't do that simple task, they should step aside and let someone else do it. ❧

HEADING THE
DIVISION OF CRIMINAL
INVESTIGATION

It was shortly after laying Craig to rest that I began getting requests from the deputy attorney general, the Management Services administrator, and other DOJ executives to consider coming back to DCI. The DCI administrator had decided to retire, and the position was going to open up.

The DCI administrator is considered one of the highest-level state law enforcement positions in Wisconsin by nature of the agency's jurisdiction and scope of mission. It was a job I would have loved but never thought I would be considered for it. Now I found it staring at me. Each time the DOJ representatives spoke with me about coming back and applying for the position, I politely declined. I had given my word to Governor Doyle to serve in the Wisconsin Emergency Management position and, to be frank, was not overly enthusiastic about going back to J.B. Van Hollen's administration based on what I had seen it do to the DCI. Not that I had anything against J.B., but I had watched as his administration seemed to be gutting my home agency.

The selection process for the DCI administrator position went on, and I did not apply. Then I received a phone call from the DOJ administrator of Management Services, who asked to have breakfast with me. She seemed dismayed that I didn't apply, as they were sure I would, knowing my commitment to the agency. I told her that I knew they had great applicants, and her reply was simply, "We didn't have any Ed Walls on the list," and the attorney general wasn't comfortable with the list he had. She went on to explain why the agency needed me and my leadership style at that time. They needed someone who would take care of their staff, lead with principle, and help the agency recover. I was flattered, but reluctant.

I finally relented and said that if Van Hollen wanted to speak with me, then we should probably meet in person and dispense with the stream of messengers. She returned with that message, and Van Hollen's secretary called to arrange a lunch the following day. It was a day I would never forget.

We met at the Brocach restaurant, downstairs from the DOJ. It was an awkward meeting because I had so many thoughts racing through my mind. J.B. was direct and to the point, which I appreciated. He said, "I need you to run the DCI, and I will do whatever I have to for that to happen." Before this time, J.B. and I were not close or even that friendly. We saw each other in the elevator or in passing, but beyond that it was simple pleasantries. What did catch my attention was that he was not asking me to come back because I owed him something, but because he felt that the agency needed me. He wanted capability and not just a political lapdog.

I reminded him that the position was a civil service position and not an appointment that he could simply make as an elected official. Of course, I thought this was likely a waste of time since he had already tried to sidestep the law on this very issue with Jim Warren. He told me he understood that, and he was willing to halt the ongoing process and start it over if I would apply. I then told him that I had accepted Governor Doyle's appointment and that I was a man of my word, even if that would keep me from applying for a job leading my home agency.

I was aware that Governor Doyle was not running again from conversations I had with him and his cabinet members. However, my word is my bond, and I would not sacrifice it. J.B. then asked if I would apply if he went and spoke with the governor, and the governor approved. I told him I would have to consider it but cautioned him that he would have to give me the latitude to run the agency and trust me to do what was right. I did not want to be micromanaged and expected him to honor the intention of the legislature with regard to the position and the agency. He agreed and spoke with Governor Doyle shortly thereafter. He called me after that meeting and told me the governor agreed.

I spoke with Governor Doyle later that day, and he reminded me he was not running for re-election, although it had not been released publicly yet. He encouraged me to pursue the DCI administrator position for my sake and my family's because he understood that it was a permanent administrator position in the agency he swore me into when he was attorney general. He also knew that my ability to remain as the Wisconsin Emergency Management administrator after his term ended was questionable at best. Ultimately, I applied for the position, competed for it through the civil service selection process, and was selected.

With a mixed sense of sadness and excitement, I found myself packing up my office after only nine months at Wisconsin Emergency Management. I was leaving the agency I had come to treasure and respect, heading back to my home agency as the DCI administrator. Discontent and anger were running rampant at the DCI due in large part to Van Hollen's attempts to change the agency's mandates, and the task to bring that all under control would not be easy.

When I arrived back at DCI, I did what I did best. I immediately went on the road and held town hall meetings at the field offices across the state to talk with staff and hear their thoughts. I did this without their supervisors present so that they could speak freely.

I had only been gone nine months, yet everyone remembered me for who I was and my history as their union representative. They needed someone to talk to. They needed to speak with the guy in charge and feel that they had been heard. The supervisors weren't very excited about the prospect of the staff talking directly to the administrator unfiltered, but the exercise was worth the effort.

After I finished my office visits, with eight pages of notes I had taken, I called all the supervisors to Madison for a meeting. This was an uncomfortable meeting for some of them because when I left the DCI for Wisconsin Emergency Management, I was their peer—a special agent in charge, separated from the administrator with bureau directors between us. Then suddenly, I was back at DCI having skipped over the director rank as the new administrator. I also knew each special agent in charge very well: their strengths and weaknesses as leaders, their communication skills, their foibles, and accomplishments. And staff members were only too happy to highlight their negatives to me as the administrator.

When we all met, I tried to put them at ease, and I explained the reason for my office visits. Our staff needed the opportunity to vent after all that had transpired. And with that venting came some observations they needed to hear about. Without calling out individual supervisors by name, I told them how staff members felt they were being treated. I ended the meeting by stressing that our agency needed to heal, and our management team needed to foster that healing by listening to, engaging, and supporting the staff in any way possible. We were forgetting who we were, as the only statewide criminal investigative agency, and what made us so remarkable.

We quickly reinstituted the DCI in-service, where all the staff came together twice a year to complete their required yearly training. It had been discontinued by the previous administrator because it was too expensive. Of course, that might have had something to do with running them at resorts and water parks. I could never understand that practice, conservative as I am. My instruction was that they be run at the Volk Field military base, where staff slept in barrack accommodations and shared bathrooms. We would then hold a pig roast at night after class on the first day, and the supervisors would kick in and buy the beer.

What the previous administrator had misunderstood was the dynamics of the training event. It was not solely to meet training requirements. It was an opportunity to bring people in the same agency, who are scattered across the state, together to rekindle the flames of camaraderie. It is too easy to get caught in a mental rut and forget that we were all part of something bigger than ourselves. We were a family. We had our differences, family squabbles, heated exchanges, and more, but at the end of the day we shared an important mission, and we needed to pull together.

One of the things I had always been passionate about was training leaders—not just promoting people and throwing them into the fire, but grooming them for the positions they were to undertake. To that end, I did a simple exercise with all 16 of the supervisors and directors. I asked each of them to write down three names of people they thought would be future leaders of our department. Surprisingly, it made some of them squirm a little. A few wanted to name more than three; others didn't want to answer at all. The problem was, some of them saw this as a trap because they would want to name their friends as opposed to who they actually thought would be leaders. Others thought it would be perceived as a judgment on their own powers of observation or motivation. I took the time to explain that I just wanted an honest list of three people they thought had the natural abilities to lead others in our agency. And I told them they could make it anonymous if they wished.

The DCI at the time had about 100 special agents. Small enough so that we all knew each other and all the personalities, skills, and abilities that each person had. Out of 16 supervisory staff, each picking three names, the list that was generated had only 14 names on it. When I told them the results, I noted that each of us saw the same thing when we honestly evaluated our staff, and that's why there was such a small number. Then I asked, "What have you done to personally mentor those people and groom others for potential leadership roles in the future?" The room was silent, and I simply said, "That was a rhetorical question, but I hope you all see where I'm going with this." They understood.

In pursuing my intention to develop leadership in those we already had, I bought a case of the book *The 21 Irrefutable Laws of Leadership* by John Maxwell. It gave many examples of leadership done correctly by real people in tough situations. When I handed out the books as Christmas presents at the monthly supervisor meeting, the supervisors and directors were all underwhelmed. By the looks on their faces, I wondered if they would have preferred crocheted oven mitts. Then I explained that each of them would be briefing the group on a chapter of the book, and I assigned chapters in order of seniority so nobody would think their chapter was a personal dig. Giving out books as Christmas presents with assignments attached was like giving your kid a new snow shovel. They knew there would be work involved.

One of the more mathematically astute supervisors said, "There are 21 chapters and only 19 supervisors and directors. What about the last two chapters?" I just smiled and said that I would brief those myself. The last two chapters were on the Law of Explosive Growth and the Law of Legacy. The presentations quickly became known as "Wall's Book Reports," but the desired effect was being achieved. When the supervisors briefed their chapters, they had to describe how it applied to the work we did and what their takeaways were from the chapters. Sometimes the struggle is not driving down the road, but rather getting into first gear.

As the months became warmer, I held a supervisors' meeting at our family's cabin on a lake in central Wisconsin. I told everyone to bring a bathing suit and told them we would be doing team-building exercises. I could see the puzzled looks on their faces and assured them that if they did not want to participate, that was okay, but they had to at least watch and learn. When they arrived, we had a campfire going, and our boat with a three-person tube was at the dock ready to go. We took groups to the center of the lake and equipped them with safety flotation gear. There would be two people on the tube at a time while I drove the boat and tried to knock them off. There were smiles all around as some thumped their chests and proclaimed, "Bring it on." Then I explained the second part of the exercise. Their job was to make sure their partner didn't fall off the tube, even if it meant that they did. This was not about self-preservation; it was about helping each other in the face of adversity and making sure the team was successful. It was a great day of team building.

As we began to rebuild the DCI's strength and clarify our agency philosophy, I did encounter some of the issues that Jim Warren had become frustrated with in the Van Hollen administration. When I met with Deputy Attorney General Ray Taffora early on, he expressed concern that the DCI was a bit "too independent" and thought that the division needed to be more tightly aligned with the attorney general. He also floated the idea of essentially eliminating the DCI and simply reclassifying the special agents as DOJ agents, rather than DCI agents. I listened carefully to Ray's thoughts and then politely explained why this would not be a good idea.

The DCI, by design and in law, was established to be above politics—an independent law enforcement entity with distinct responsibilities that could include criminal investigation of politicians, potentially, even the attorney general. In fact, during the caucus scandal a few years prior, the AG herself had to be firewalled from DCI's investigations during that case. That was done specifically because she was a politician and her party representatives were being investigated. I told Ray that erasing the historical, widely accepted, nonpartisan, and detached reputation the DCI had earned would be a mistake. It would give the appearance—which would likely become reality—that the only law enforcement agency tasked with statewide criminal jurisdiction was just some kind of political weapon in the hands of the AG.

I also explained that many law enforcement officers aspired to work at the DCI because of its independent reputation. We were known to be the preeminent criminal investigative agency in the state, and that was what attracted people to our ranks. I told him that it would be a mistake to simply dismiss roughly 50 years of exemplary work by branding them the AG's personal storm troopers. Ultimately, I persuaded them to leave the DCI intact. The only compromise I made was to have the DOJ reflected on our agency's logo and badges. But the efforts to reconstitute the agency into an enforcement arm of the AG gave me pause. Deep inside, I felt there was an intention rooted in politics that could render my agency as nothing more than political tool for the party in control of the AG's office.

When J.B. Van Hollen was first elected as the new AG, he rode in as the only Republican to win a major office that year. That made him, by default, the darling of the state GOP and certainly helped inflate his ego and standing across the state. He was good at the stump speech and knew how to connect one-on-one with people. J.B. and I spent a good deal of time together after I became administrator. I remember the first time he was going to be riding with me to an event, and I went to meet him in the parking garage. His assistant, Dean Stensberg, came to the garage with him and opened the back door as if the AG was going to ride in the back seat. I quickly asked, "What are you doing?" and Dean said he was helping get the attorney general into his seat. Honest and straightforward was all I knew how to be, so I replied, "I'm his administrator, not his driver. If he's riding with me, he sits up front."

J.B. looked at Dean and said, "Well, I guess he told you," and laughed while getting into the front seat. Even though I didn't like politicians much, J.B. and I got along.

As the DCI turned the corner and staff began settling into a new normal, I drew up plans to change my executive team to better align with the needs of the department. At that time, we had the administrator and four director positions in the executive team, each overseeing a bureau. Through my experience, I found as an agency head that you needed to identify a second-in-command. If you did not have an identified second-in-command, you often found that all the directors

HEADING THE DIVISION OF CRIMINAL INVESTIGATION

thought of themselves as the second-in-command and shuffled to see who could be closest to the administrator for the nod. The shuffling itself was a distraction and left people wondering who was the administrator's favorite.

Ultimately, I restructured the division's command structure and promoted one of the directors into the newly created deputy administrator position. I had known Dave Matthews since I came to the DCI. He was a critical thinker, very intelligent, and good at administrative functions, which is what I wanted. My heart was in the field with the troops and building relationships across the state and country. Dave and I balanced each other out well. He wasn't as affable as I was, but he was superb at the budget and managing the in-house administrative issues.

Things improved at the DCI, and a sense of unity began to develop once again. We were busy as always and needed more help than we had. During my tenure at DCI as administrator, J.B. let me do my job and trusted my judgment in running the agency. He was also instrumental in getting us additional funding to add more special agents and civilian staff to help carry the burden of a greatly expanding amount of work.

From an agency standpoint, we had no complaints about J.B. or how he associated with us. He attended all the DCI in-service functions for the pig roasts and, at my urging, brought other members of his executive team with him. Initially, J.B. was apprehensive about coming to the DCI in-services because he knew that the actions of his administration were still raw with the agents. He was seen as the demon that removed Jim Warren, who most people would have followed through the gates of hell. It took a lot of talking on my part to our staff to try and heal those wounds.

During those in-service gatherings, I would encourage staff to talk with J.B. and his executive staff without me nearby to share their hopes, express their concerns, and ask questions. They could talk over a beer and tell him what was on their mind or mention problems they had with my leadership without fear of retaliation, the same way I had spoken with agents without their supervisors present. They needed to know that I welcomed that kind of interaction if my efforts were going to be meaningful.

J.B. was smart enough that he surrounded himself with a good team of people. Ray Taffora ran a tight ship as deputy attorney general. Ray and I established a good relationship, and he let me run the division, free of interference. We had executive staff meetings every Monday morning in the AG's conference room, and the team got along very well—albeit, often without J.B. around. Although J.B. was good about letting us do our jobs, I got the sense that this was more connected to his being somewhat averse to being in the office rather than a guiding leadership principle.

This was not a revelation to anyone on his executive staff who knew he was often "out and about." I learned from career staff at the U.S. Attorney's Office that he had garnered the same reputation when he served as the U.S. attorney for the Western District of Wisconsin. In his duties as attorney general, J.B. made the appearances he had to make and did the occasional drive-by at DOJ headquarters. More often than not, he was missing in action, and that was just fine with those of us on the inside doing the work. The best supervisors I ever had just let me do my job.

As J.B.'s personal assistant, Dean Stensberg had made himself indispensable to politicians over the years. He was Tommy Thompson's assistant before joining J.B. and would get himself put into a variety of state positions by garnering favor through personal service. I will never forget going to J.B.'s residence to pick him up for a meeting. J.B. came to the door, and I looked past him to see Dean inside vacuuming the living room! That was how Dean worked. He ingratiated himself to his boss and then dug in like a wood tick. He proudly told me of the clothes and other personal items he had purchased for J.B. and his family. He was the preeminent gentleman's butler and confidant. I couldn't help but wonder if that was in the state job description. As the saying went amongst DOJ administrators, who all had a clear understanding of Dean's role, "Everyone should have a Dean." As I write this book, Dean once again found his way into a highly placed personal assistant position—this time working for the chief justice of the Wisconsin Supreme Court.

There was a day when J.B.'s absenteeism issues came crashing to the forefront by way of an open records request. Todd Richmond, a reporter from the Associated Press, had filed a request for J.B.'s security card swipe records, which would have shown how often he was actually in the DOJ building. There was a thunderclap of anxiety as J.B.'s Achilles' heel was about to be plastered in the paper. J.B. was at that meeting where this was discussed, and he was very concerned.

In response to Richmond's open records request, Dean started throwing out defenses on why there would be so few card swipes. Things like, "He is always with a staffer that swipes the door for him." With regard to the lack of meetings that would be on his calendar to explain the absences, Dean suggested that his scheduler did not put everything on J.B.'s calendars, and that made the nervous twitches in the room only increase. All the while, J.B.'s eyes were darting around the room, and he became more concerned as the discussion continued. Afterward, I would hear that Dean went so far as to take J.B.'s card to swipe in and out around the DOJ to make it look like J.B. was in the office and wandering the building. I recall thinking to myself as this mini-drama was unfolding, "Why not just come to work like the rest of us?" Fortunately, for J.B., Richmond never followed up on those requests, and he had no idea of the turmoil he caused. I always wondered what those swipe records would have looked like before and after the open records request. The contrast would have been stark.

As a special agent in charge and as administrator, I was responsible for overseeing the purchase of our vehicle fleet, which was about 100 units. When J.B. came into office, I had a newer Chrysler 300 taken from the DCI fleet and assigned to him for his state-issued vehicle. He had that vehicle for a short time when he had occasion to ride with me in my state-issued Tahoe, which was full of law enforcement gear, radios, sirens, etc. He asked me if he could get a vehicle like mine. We had already made the vehicle purchase for that year through the Department of Administration (DOA), and the purchase period was closed. He said he wanted something like the governor had (Chevy Suburban), but not quite as big in deference to the position. I told him I would see what I could do.

I contacted the DOA and advised them that the attorney general wanted a Tahoe for his position. Since the vehicle buy had already been made, DOA advised that they could lease him one on the state contract, which they did. It was a very nice silver Tahoe, well equipped with leather seats and a good radio. I had it brought to DOJ headquarters and placed in his parking space. J.B. seemed very happy with it. However, Dean Stensberg was not. He advised that the attorney general would not be seen being driven around in that "gaudy rig" and told me to find a place for it in the DCI fleet. I explained that we wouldn't order a vehicle this well equipped, and he was unmoved. I was amazed that Dean had somehow garnered the amount of power he seemed to throw around. We ended up assigning the vehicle to the SAC of the Milwaukee field office to keep the mileage low until the lease was up.

Meanwhile, Dean decided he would go one step farther and had J.B. announce he was, in fact, turning in his state vehicle to "save tax-payers money." The story was reported across the state as J.B. took bows for being so conservative. What they didn't mention was that af-ter that announcement, the DCI was repeatedly tasked with supply-ing a special agent driver and vehicle to haul him around. We failed to see the cost savings in that move, which would become known as the "Driving Miss Daisy" assignment for those tasked with driving J.B. around. In fact, it seemed more like an attitude of entitlement that we had never seen in any attorneys general before.

My philosophy as a leader, regardless of the agency I led, has always been influenced by a 360-degree view as to what was going on. However, the more dictatorial-minded typically hated that mindset. At one meeting I was running, I told my staff I wanted input from a particular group of people who would be impacted by one of our proposed actions, and one of the supervisors blurted out, "With all due respect, why do we have to do that? We aren't running a democracy here."

I paused a few moments and then looked up slowly and said, "Okay, you are right. We will just act unilaterally without input from those affected."

The supervisor smiled and said, "Good. Thank you."

After another few moments of pause, I looked at him again and said, "With that, I'm transferring you to a different position where you won't be interacting with staff, and your new salary will be 15 percent lower."

His mouth fell agape, and the tension in the room was throbbing like a jugular vein. He then replied, "Why? What did I do wrong? How can you do this to me?"

I looked at him and said very matter-of-factly, "Those are probably the very same questions people will be asking us when we act without input and force a decision on them. Would you have wanted input on my decision to transfer you and cut your pay?"

He lowered his head and simply said, "Point taken." He kept his position but lost his attitude.

When I was the special agent in charge in the Investigative Services Bureau, I had occasion to be the supervisor on scene at several high-profile crime responses. All of them left impressions that changed the way I did my job and how I would respond in the future. That's not unusual, because lessons are always learned in law enforcement work. If you think you've stopped learning, then it's time to retire.

I will never forget responding on September 29, 2006, to Weston High School for a report of an active shooter with shots fired and people wounded. I just happened to be closer than anyone else from DCI at that time, as I was in route to a meeting in that general area. This was the first case I had responded to where an active shooter was potentially involved, and information was being received painfully slowly as I raced to the scene. On arrival, I was advised that the suspect, a student named Eric Hainstock, had shot the principal, John Klang, and was in custody. The principal had been transported to the hospital, and his condition was unknown on my arrival.

As I think back on that day, there was one thought that kept racing through my mind as I looked around at the shock, horror, and fear on people's faces and the blood smeared on the shiny school floors. This was one kid with a gun he took from home. What if this had been someone determined to cause death and destruction for a different ideology? What if a well-armed and prepared terrorist should target a school? These were thoughts we had always kept on our dashboard with the Homeland Security Council, but it was different standing there looking at the devastation that had resulted. This was not a hypothesis or a tabletop exercise. It sent chills down my spine, and unfortunately, I would see those fears realized too many times in the coming years.

Another case that shaped me was the horrific Crandon multiple homicide case in Forest County. The call came at about 3:30 a.m. on October 7, 2007, and I was advised that a Forest County deputy had gone on a killing spree in Crandon. He was still on the loose, and I was to head toward the scene with a cell-tracking team to do what we could in locating him. The suspect, Tyler Peterson, was a 20-year-old deputy and a member of the regional SWAT team. The prospect of hunting down a deputy with SWAT training left a cold feeling in my stomach as I headed northeast.

The DCI's tactical team had also been activated and was heading toward the scene from all corners of the state. As I continued toward the scene, details began to trickle in: six people dead and another critically wounded. Gunman still on the loose. The victims were his friends. Possibly a girlfriend issue. The crime scene is bad. Need more people.

Ultimately, through cellular tracking technology, we were able to pinpoint Peterson's location at a rural residence in Crandon. SAC Jed Sperry was also sent to Crandon, and he took control of the initial crime scene. When I arrived at the blockaded intersection a few hundred yards from the location where Peterson was located, I was met by the Forest County chief deputy, who was obviously distraught. He asked if I was with the DCI. I answered that I was, and he asked if I was a boss. And again, I said I was. He then exclaimed, "You have to take over. We are too close to this. He was one of ours." I told him I understood and would assume command. I walked toward the police car where the topographical maps were being laid out on the hood. I was advised that two of the regional SWAT team snipers had managed to get into position and had their scopes on Peterson.

We had determined that Peterson was at the residence with five other people he also considered his friends—not very encouraging considering what he had done to his other friends. Text messages were being received from a couple of the people with Peterson by another friend, which were being relayed to us at the hastily established command post. The texts indicated that Peterson was armed with a scoped hunting rifle, but it was placed up against the building as he sat on the porch. However, he was still wearing his sidearm. The texting friend advised that Peterson had been drunk at the time of the shooting and was now coming to the realization of what he had done. It was a very tenuous situation, and the weight of deciding how to best resolve it was heavy.

Just then, the chief deputy who had been walking away suddenly turned and exclaimed, "If they have him in their sights, they need to shoot him right now!"

I was shocked to hear this, and I was afraid the SWAT commander would take it as an order, so I quickly told the commander, "That is NOT the order." I knew that with the spectacle of a deputy who had killed six people, our actions would be judged in perfect hindsight, and I wanted to make sure we handled this properly.

I calmly said to the commander, "This is your shoot order. If he puts his hand on his gun, shoot him. If he runs for cover or toward the woods with a gun, shoot him. If it looks like the situation is deteriorating and the others are in imminent danger, shoot him." The commander acknowledged the order and relayed it to his snipers. There was a chill up my spine knowing that I had just given a shoot order that could involve killing a cop. But he was a cop no longer; he was now a murderer who had left his oath behind. Meanwhile, the DCI tactical team was arriving, and they quickly started to assemble for insertion into the area. The regional Bear Cat armored vehicle was there, and the team would approach in that.

The team started the Bear Cat and began to mount up. The diesel engine Bear Cat had a distinct sound when it started up, and we would surmise later after speaking with the people he had been with that the deputy heard it, realizing what was about to happen. Suddenly, the radio crackled, and the sniper reported that Peterson had broken from the group and was running toward the woods with his handgun in his hand. I dropped my head, knowing what was coming, and a moment later the shot rang out. Then pistol shots could be heard. I motioned the SWAT team to move in, and they started quickly driving up the road. The sniper called out that shots were being fired by Peterson, and they assumed he was returning fire. Then the shots stopped and all was silent. I jumped into my Tahoe and started up the road behind the team, pulling on my tactical vest.

The team immediately broke into a search pattern, heading toward the last known area Peterson had been in. In just a few moments, one of the team members called out, "Shooter down, over here." Peterson had apparently tried to shoot himself twice, but flinched and just wounded himself. The third shot was effective, and the incident ended. The sniper had done what he had been trained to do, hitting Peterson on the run at over a hundred yards. His shot brought Peterson down and left him to make his final decision. I could not imagine what the sniper felt as he had Peterson in his sights, knowing he was about to shoot someone he knew, trained with, and likely considered a friend. The weight of these decisions and actions are long-lasting for everyone involved.

It was tragic. The small sheriff's department was shattered, and the community was left reeling. Ultimately, they tore down the house where the initial carnage had occurred in an effort to put the bad memories behind them. My takeaway from the event was the importance of getting help as fast as possible to law enforcement agencies that had suffered a violent loss. The emotion of the moment could easily overtake leaders who are under incredible stress.

Another tragic incident: It was about 7:00 a.m. on Sunday, March 21, 2011, and I was the DCI administrator. We were up with our family at our cabin in central Wisconsin. I was in the shower when my wife walked in and said, "Tony Barthuly is on the phone. An officer has been shot." Tony was the Fond du Lac police chief and a good friend of mine. He was one of the most sincere and thoughtful people I had ever known, and he was obviously shaken. Tony explained that one of his officers had been killed, another was critically wounded, and their K-9 had also been shot. The crime scene was expansive, the shooter was still active, and they needed help. I told him we were on the way.

I immediately called my bureau directors and told them to start calling agents out to respond. In total, the DCI sent about 30 agents and two directors to the scene. When I arrived, the shooter had already been neutralized, but the scene was still hectic. Our agents had spread across a four-block crime scene, and multiple cars and houses had been shot up during the wild fusillade of gunfire that erupted on that cold March morning. People were in a daze at the Fond du Lac Police Department. I found Tony and just hugged him for a minute; he was trembling. Losing an officer is one of the worst scenarios any chief can go through. It reminds all of us just how vulnerable we are and how precarious reaching the end of our shifts can be.

When I saw J.B. later, he asked what kind of response we provided, and I told him. He pulled his head back and said, "Thirty agents? Really?" he asked. "Why so many?" I explained that when one police officer has been killed and another wounded and the shooter is still active, a robust response is necessary. I also noted that several of the department's vehicles had been shot, many of their patrol rifles had been fired, and the accounting for the dozens of bullets fired by the suspect and law enforcement would all take staff time. When you shut down entire neighborhoods to process crime scenes, it takes time and inconveniences everyone.

No cop likes to have their gun taken away when an investigation is being conducted into a shooting incident. It leaves them feeling naked and exposed. I instructed our agents that for every long gun we took from officers for testing, I wanted them to turn over their DCI-issued long gun for the Fond du Lac Police Department to use until the weapons could be cleared and documented. Their patrol officers were far more likely to need long guns than our agents, and it would only be temporary.

Likewise, the county sheriff started making calls to round up spare law enforcement vehicles in the area to loan the department until Fond du Lac's could be documented and repaired. That is how cops work. We share the same basic needs and work quickly to fill the voids.

When J.B. and I attended the funeral, the mayor of Fond du Lac came up to J.B. and me, thanking us for everything we had done for his city. He was particularly overwhelmed by the number of people we sent and the effort we took to bring order out of the chaos. As he walked away, J.B. turned to me and said, "I won't question your responses again. Nice work."

J.B. was receiving a lot of pressure from the Republican Party to run for governor in 2010, but he wasn't inclined to do so. He was too involved with his family and did not want to take on the role of governor. I think he regretted that decision afterward because he had the name recognition and a good record to run on. The truth is, I don't think he could have handled the job. He was just averse to heavy workloads and too content to let business take care of itself.

Instead, J.B. decided to run for re-election as attorney general, and Scott Walker, who was Milwaukee County executive, decided to run for governor and won the Republican nomination. During the campaign, Milwaukee County District Attorney John Chisholm's office had started a John Doe investigation into some missing funds and possible campaign donation violations involving Walker's staff.

The news of the investigation was being covered prominently in the press.

The day before the election, I received a call from Chisholm. John was, without a doubt, one of the best prosecutors I ever worked with. He was well balanced, thoughtful, and determined. He had handled many cases that I had been involved with on cell tracking, homicides, and drug cases, and I always respected him. However, during the ongoing John Doe investigation, I recall thinking that politics were seeping into the process, and I never thought of John as a political partisan.

John told me that he was working on a case through a John Doe investigation that could involve criminal charges against Walker or his staff or both. He could not go into details because of the secrecy order involved but wanted to know if the DCI could execute search warrants his investigators had prepared that very night, on election eve. He stated the warrants would be for documents and data relating to the investigation.

I was somewhat shocked that John was proposing this and told him that I felt the timing was ill-advised since there was no exigency that he had offered. It had the appearance that someone was trying to influence the election, where the news would be blasted across the front page as citizens went to the polls the next day. I told John that we would not execute the search warrants and urged him to wait a day so he would not be accused of trying to affect the election results.

John insisted that he was going to execute the warrants that night and then asked if I could at least provide DCI special agents to be posted outside for scene security. I ultimately agreed to provide special agents for security, but we would not be involved in entering the scenes, executing the warrants, or seizing evidence. The warrants were executed, computers and documents seized, and the press ate it up.

Despite all the publicity surrounding the John Doe investigation, Scott Walker was elected governor, and both houses went to the Republicans. It was the first time since 1998 that the Republicans controlled the governor's office and both houses. What was unique in this election was that the Republicans also controlled the attorney general's office, as J.B. coasted to re-election, making it a clean sweep of all major offices and agencies for the GOP.

This created a pervasive feeling of invincibility among Republican officials. Their chests were puffed out, and they had a swagger in their step. Personally, I preferred an electorate that was not one-sided for either party. Why? It meant that compromise was required. Therefore, solutions would probably better reflect the will of the people.

In the aftermath of Election Day, I had the feeling that something was coming with this sweeping, broad control. Too many people wanted to plant their spears in the corpse of the Democrats, who had been vanquished so handily. There were promises of big, bold actions to come. I would never have guessed what they were, but I would soon find out. ◗

INTO THE STORM

The DCI had historically done the background investigations for governors-elect appointees, and we offered that service to the incoming Walker team. My deputy administrator, Dave Matthews, took the lead in coordinating the work, which was spread across the state to agents in the various field offices. Like every transition, we had to sometimes deliver news that certain appointees had problems in their background that should preclude them from an appointment. Typically, I had those conversations personally with the governor's transition director, John Hiller.

Sometimes those conversations about potential appointees being problematic were difficult. In some cases, the governor-elect would bypass recommendations made in the background investigations, but that was their prerogative. Most often, the hang-ups involved financial dealings, domestic disputes, or other tawdry behavior.

One day when I went down to talk with John about a potential appointee issue, he casually asked what I thought about the secretary of the Department of Corrections position. I told him I had a great recommendation for him, but I couldn't take the position because I was in my probationary period as a civil service administrator. If I left during that time, I would have no restoration rights, and besides that, I loved my job. Aside from my family, there was nothing more important than my job as DCI administrator.

Ultimately, the governor appointed Gary Hamblin, the retired Dane County sheriff, who had also served with the DCI for many years. At that time, Gary was administrator of the Law Enforcement Services Division in the DOJ. Gary was a good man, steady-handed and always calm. He was a great choice for DOC secretary.

As January was approaching, I was asked if I would like to attend the Governor's Inaugural Ball with my wife. The tickets would be free. I thought it might be nice to at least attend something like that at least once, but I would not accept free tickets. Instead, I purchased the tickets online under my wife's maiden name to avoid being tied politically to anyone. Unfortunately, that led to a constant stream of political donation requests that we still can't seem to stop, since Walker sold his donation list. It was a nice event, and there was a good picture taken of the governor with my wife and me. Beyond that, I wanted to stay away from the politics.

During the transition period, as the DCI was conducting the backgrounds on Walker's potential appointees, District Attorney John Chisholm reached out to me again with regard to the John Doe investigation. He asked to meet with me and the AG to discuss some new information. I told him I would set up the meeting and get back to him.

When I met with Deputy Attorney General Ray Taffora to schedule the meeting, he was very concerned. Ray and I had discussed the possibility that they may want the DCI to get involved at some point in the John Doe investigation. Ray feared that J.B. would want to take the investigation out of a sense of duty and asked that I help convince J.B. otherwise. I had good reasons not to want my agency involved in this quagmire. We were already stretched to the breaking point with our constant stream of high-profile cases and now had all the background investigations we were doing for the governor-elect. Getting involved in the John Doe investigation would cripple our abilities to deliver on the mission of the agency as opposed to getting weighed down in a political fight.

Subsequently, John and his deputy, Kent Lovern, came to meet with J.B., Deputy Attorney General Taffora, and me. There was some noticeable tension in the air as the Democratic DA came to meet with the freshly reminted attorney general, who was now part of the overwhelming Republican majority. John and Kent explained what they had found so far in their investigation and indicated that further investigations may be launched soon. They pointed to the fact that the Walker staff at the Milwaukee County executive's office had set up a "covert computer system" that they felt was being used during county work hours to do campaign work. As I listened to this, I recall thinking that *every* person in politics was likely doing campaign work on the taxpayer's dime, because the only thing they seemed concerned with was getting re-elected. On top of that, we had real crime to investigate, and political shenanigans were not high on my critical to-do list.

The question was asked if it was possible that the alternative computer network was set up specifically so that people could work on their own time, like on breaks or during lunch, and not on government computers so they wouldn't be violating the laws with regard to campaign work being done on county time. The answer was that it was not likely, based on other information they had revealed in the investigation.

John asked that I "firewall" some of my agents and assign them to his office to conduct the current and upcoming investigations. I explained that my feeling was that it would be difficult, if not impossible, given how overloaded we were. I asked John if he had considered referring the case to the FBI or the U.S. attorney. If the case was as he described, then those agencies could certainly have jurisdiction. He replied that he had not and wanted to retain control of the cases. We listened to the rest of the information they could share and advised that we would discuss it internally before getting back to them.

After John and Kent left, we returned to the AG's conference room and had a frank conversation. As Ray feared, J.B. said that he felt he "had to" conduct the investigation and went into his reasons on why he should. He pointed to instances where he had been asked to investigate Jim Doyle and was concerned that people would paint him as partisan if he turned the case away. Ray, Tommy Thompson's former legal chief, was absolutely against the DOJ getting involved. He pointed out to J.B. that for the first time in many years, the Republicans controlled all the high offices, and his involvement could fracture the GOP at a time when they finally obtained the control they had been after for years. He also pointed out that it could permanently harm the relationship between the governor and the attorney general in the coming years

It was the epitome of political pressure. The top state law enforcement official, a Republican, deciding if he would investigate the governor, also a Republican, based on the request of a Democratic district attorney. It was truly a no-win situation. If he decided not to investigate, then he was a partisan hack protecting his political friend. If he did investigate, he would be the pariah of his beloved Republican Party for upsetting the power base that had just swept into office.

In an email that I wrote, which popped up in a newspaper article later, I stated that from my standpoint, "This is one to try and stay away from. I can't see any good coming from it." Our division would be whipsawed as we had been during the investigations into the caucus scandal, and the atmosphere of political persuasion would permeate everything we would do. I felt strongly that the DCI should not be used as a weaponized enforcement arm for politicians to chase each other for political gain. In my mind, the case should have been handled by the feds.

Ultimately, Ray was successful in convincing J.B. not to investigate the case. Ray drafted the letter that was subsequently sent to Chisholm turning down his request, which was designed to give J.B.

cover from attacks. It did not, and the press went after J.B., claiming he was protecting Walker.

The issues revealed through the course of the John Doe investigations are important for multiple reasons, but in my own case, they were instructive in how Scott Walker and his staff would view email and communications. They took a militant attitude that emails and written communications were bad, which I would not experience until after I became a cabinet secretary. This was very likely because of the John Doe investigations and the way those communications were wrapped around the necks of Walker's staff members who would ultimately be convicted.

Admittedly, when I first heard of the first John Doe investigation, it seemed purely partisan. The idea that Walker and his staff had intentionally set up a secondary computer system to make sure they were abiding by the laws seemed plausible. However, as my time in the cabinet grew, and I watched the way they handled communications and the constant veiled secrecy, I concluded that the allegations that he and his campaign staff intentionally tried to get around the law were likely true. That was a painful conclusion to come to because I had to admit to myself that my first impression of the man was wrong. I wanted Scott Walker to be different. I wanted him to be above the usual fray of political ambition and the "ends justify the means" mentality that was so prevalent in politics.

As a cop, I had learned to trust my gut. I could not count the number of times that simple premise had saved me. We prided ourselves on being able to read people—their actions, physical cues, their eyes, their speech, their furtive movements, changing stories, nervousness—all of it. My wife would often accuse me of being overly suspicious of people, but she doesn't look at things the same way as I do. She is loving, trusting, giving, and sees the best in everyone. Then again, she has never been hit from behind or attacked by the person standing in front of her who, just a moment before, offered no clue as to what was coming.

In law enforcement, we were always taught to be aware of our surroundings, to recognize things that could become weapons in an instant, and to know where the exits were. We were taught to look at the eyes; they are the windows to the soul. Watch the hands; they are the delivery method. Be hypervigilant; don't become complacent. And understand that no two situations are the same. In the blink of an eye, things can go from run-of-the-mill to life-threatening. Always be prepared and make it home at the end of your shift.

All this training would be useless in dealing with Scott Walker. Why? Because he was unpretentious and seemed so friendly. That had the effect of neutralizing your self-protection instincts and training. Scott Walker is an easy guy to like and an easy guy to talk to. He could strike up a conversation on almost anything, and you felt like he was truly listening to you. He would look you in the eye when he spoke and practiced a form of "appreciative inquiry" that I had learned in college years before. He would ask about you and your family to make that connection, and you walked away thinking, "What a great guy!"

As all the hullabaloo over the election and the first John Doe investigation was playing out in the media, we at the DCI continued doing our background investigations for Walker's appointments. During that time, we began to catch wind of an action the governor was considering that had something to do with big changes to civil service and public-sector unions, and I thought, "Good luck with that!" Having previously been on the union's executive board, co-chaired the bargaining committee in contract negotiations, and been involved in the union establishing political action committees, I thought it would never happen. I knew firsthand what power those unions wielded. My eyes were soon to be opened wide. ❧

THE ACT 10
BOMBSHELL

When I first saw the proposal, I honestly wasn't that surprised. Anyone who had read about Walker's history in Milwaukee County knew about the open warfare he had engaged in with the unions there, and this certainly seemed like a score he wanted to settle. He had been frustrated by contracts, union money going to his adversaries, limitations on his ability to do what he wanted, and the tedious work of negotiation. Throughout Walker's terms, he was all about declarations and not negotiations.

Act 10 required public employees to pay a percentage of their health care costs, required them to pay a percentage of their pension contributions, and prohibited their unions from bargaining over anything other than wages, which in any event would not be allowed to rise over the rate of inflation. On top of that, every public-sector union would be required to have an annual recertification election, and to stay alive, the union would need to get at least 50 percent of the votes of all its members, not just those who showed up to vote. Imagine if politicians were elected that way! It seemed at the start to intentionally place insurmountable obstacles ahead of the unions.

I was angry with how the law enforcement exemptions cut my own people out of the picture. It seemed obvious that the State Patrol was exempted because they provided the governor's security detail. It had already been a political football when Walker appointed Steve Fitzgerald as the State Patrol's superintendent, since he was the father of two leaders in the legislature who would be instrumental in pushing through his Act 10 legislation. Now it looked like the State Patrol was granted special favors to make Walker's life easier.

Since I was in frequent contact with John Hiller, the transition director, and Keith Gilkes, the governor's chief of staff, I wasted no time in calling them to express my displeasure. The response was essentially, "Sorry, it's a done deal." I told them both it was unfair and would set up a divisive atmosphere for state law enforcement officers. They were not concerned.

That night, the next day, and for weeks to follow, anger flowed into the streets around the capitol as protestors flocked to the area. The protests and civil disobedience were historic and got worldwide attention. My office overlooked the capitol, and I stood there watching day after day as people filled the streets. It was a display of democracy and civil discourse without violence. The air pulsated with shouts and chants that reverberated through the walls of our building. The capitol looked like it was under siege. The only things missing were the trebuchets positioned around the perimeter and archers on the walls.

On one of the first days of the protests, I looked out my office window and saw a big Ryder truck driving slowly up Martin Luther King Jr. Boulevard, picking its way through the undulating ocean of protestors in its path, onto the south side driveway and right up to within 30 feet of the capitol. A guy with long hair hopped out of the cab, went to the back of the truck, checked the padlock on the door, and just walked away. I felt a cold rush race up my spine.

The Wisconsin State Capitol is one of the largest in the country, and its dome is second in size only to the U.S. Capitol. If someone, or some group, wanted to make a very public and violent statement about our country, our beliefs, our politics, or just about anything else, here was an opportunity, with tens of thousands of protestors, the media all around, in front of a building that resembled the U.S. Capitol. And a guy just walked away from a large truck and disappeared into the crowd. All I could think of was Oklahoma City.

We quickly notified law enforcement and our special agents working undercover in the crowds to try and locate the driver. We couldn't risk a stampede of protestors, but we also couldn't risk a bomb going off. For several minutes, it was extremely tense as we waited to see if the driver could be located. Fortunately, we found him, and he came back to the truck to unlock the back for inspection. The big truck was full of sound equipment for the union rallies. Crisis averted.

As the unexpected size of the protests grew, Department of Administration Secretary Mike Huebsch put together a law enforcement executive group. I was asked to join that group to represent the DOJ and DCI. Also, in that group were Capitol Police Chief Charles Tubbs, State Patrol Superintendent Steve Fitzgerald, DNR Chief Warden Randy Stark, Madison Police Chief Noble Wray, Dane County Sheriff Dave Mahoney, and UW Police Chief Sue Riseling.

An Incident Command System was put into place, and the various agencies were assigned responsibilities. The Madison Police Department announced that they would not be entering the capitol grounds to support law enforcement but would instead patrol the perimeter off state property. Likewise, Sheriff Dave Mahoney declared that his deputies would not serve as "palace guards" for an uprising he disagreed with. Political barriers were erected across the thin blue line.

The action of politicizing their position by some on the law enforcement executive committee was not completely unexpected or surprising, considering the well-known liberal political climate in the greater Madison area. However, from a "law enforcement brotherhood" position, it was disappointing. The influence of political bias and pandering for public affection had corrupted the thin blue line. The concern was not so much on helping protect each other and the public, as it was on getting favorable news coverage and appreciation from protestors and voters. To each their own, but it would affect decisions made down the road.

The publicity surrounding Chief Tubbs and Chief Riseling's interaction with the protestors to keep everyone calm had caused some concern within the governor's office. It was thought the chiefs might be leaking information to protestors, as it seemed the protestors knew what the police were going to do before we did it. Then again, we may not have been in that situation if someone had taken the time to talk with people.

With tens of thousands of protestors descending on the capitol daily, it quickly became obvious that more police would be needed. Having previously run Wisconsin Emergency Management, I knew that we needed to activate its Emergency Police Services section. This agreement, authorized by state law, allowed for the activation of mutual aid declarations, which could draw upon law enforcement agencies across the state to send personnel. It granted those responding officers jurisdictional authority and guaranteed payment of the cost of their services to their home agencies.

Emergency Police Services is an incredible asset for the state. As I explained it to Secretary Huebsch, he was impressed with the capability. He asked, "What will that cost?"

I simply replied, "It isn't cheap, but we have no choice." The system was activated, and law enforcement from across the state was pulled to Madison. The logistics of this type of operation were enormous. It involved arranging for lodging, meals, back-filling positions at the home agency, and a myriad of other challenges. Within a few days, we had 700 officers a day committed to the mission.

From DCI, we devoted all our resources initially, with many of our undercover agents from the Narcotics Bureau infiltrating the protest groups. It was kind of funny to be walking around the capitol, with protest groups initially heckling anyone in a suit, and seeing my agents screaming and waving signs at me. They just grinned and took the opportunity to egg on their boss while incognito.

THE ACT 10 BOMBSHELL

A few days later, Secretary Huebsch and I found ourselves in court to testify on the state's request to close the capitol. As we sat there in the courtroom waiting for the judge, Mike turned to me and said, "If we don't get this under control, I bet this could cost the state a couple of million dollars for law enforcement."

I just looked at him and raised my eyebrows, saying, "It's going to be more than that—a lot more." I sent a few text messages to our fusion center staff for numbers of officers working, did some simple math, and told Mike a few minutes later that my guess was this response would cost the state over $10 million when it was all said and done.

He was shocked and said, "Are you kidding me?" My estimate was low, as it ended up being over $12 million when it was all over.

On February 17, 2011, there was to be a vote to pass Act 10, and the protests were reaching a fevered pitch. By this time, I was using the tunnel between the DOJ and the capitol daily to move around because the crowds were so thick. Plans to move the legislature after the vote were put in place by law enforcement, and we braced for the impact. But it wouldn't come that day, as 14 Democratic legislators fled the state to block the vote. I just laughed to myself when I saw the lengths to which politicians would go to grandstand.

Huebsch was angry that the legislators had fled. Having been the previous speaker of the assembly, he saw this as a particular gross violation of the legislators' responsibilities. Mike called me to a meeting with him, the governor's chief of staff, Keith Gilkes, and Deputy Chief of Staff Eric Schutt. Mike asked me if the DCI still had the cell tracking equipment I had told him about previously, and I answered that we did.

He then asked if I could use that equipment and go into Illinois to track the footloose legislators, take them into custody, and bring them back to Wisconsin. I smiled and looked down at the floor. When I looked up, I said, "I'm guessing that you want me to drag them onto the floor of the assembly with hoods over their heads, drop them to their knees, and dramatically pull off their hoods in time for the speaker to call the vote."

It lightened the mood for a moment, but I could tell that my overly visual depiction was probably not that far off by the smiles on their faces. Before they could answer, I followed up by saying, "Yes, we can do that ... but unfortunately it's called kidnapping. Absent a court order from Wisconsin that would be accepted in Illinois, we can't help." That did start an internal conversation with the governor's office and their lawyers about possibly getting a court order, but it never ended up moving forward.

On a couple of occasions, I received word from Mike that the legislators were coming back or going to meet and talk, but then nothing would happen. I found out later that some covert rendezvous did occur, but no real progress was made. It all felt like a cheap spy novel as negotiations were underway to lure them back. Ultimately, the Republicans controlled the legislature, and they found a way to pass the portion of the bill pertaining to collective bargaining changes without the "Fab 14," as the wayward Democratic senators were dubbed in the media.

Throughout the protests, I had many occasions to walk and talk with Secretary Huebsch. I liked Mike, and we became friendly during those tumultuous times. Late one night, we were looking down from the railings on the second floor of the capitol at the center of the rotunda below. Sleeping bags, blankets, and bodies were covering almost every square foot. The protests had become a democracy pajama party as they refused to lose their toehold in the building. Then we saw something odd. Down below us, under a pile of blankets, there was a rhythm of physical undulation taking place. Mike looked at me and asked, "What is going on over there?"

I smiled and said, "That, my friend, is someone making protest babies." He was horrified at the couple procreating on the capitol's rotunda floor. We were the only ones who appeared to notice. Everyone else was asleep.

In the early evening of March 9, 2011, after control of the capitol had been re-established, I received an urgent call from Mike.

THE ACT 10 BOMBSHELL

He told me that the Senate would be holding an unexpected vote shortly on a partitioned part of the Act 10 bill. His concern was that he had just released all the extra law enforcement officers who had been on duty because all was quiet. Shortly after we spoke, the protestors began appearing out of nowhere, alerted by social media of the actions about to be undertaken by the legislature. They were running up the side streets, from the buildings, from everywhere. It was a stampede. I couldn't help but wonder how they all knew so fast. A lesson in social media effectiveness. They rushed toward the capitol, and I watched from my office as they stormed the doors and could be seen climbing through windows. Democratic legislators were opening their office windows and helping people get inside the building. They then rushed to open the doors from the inside, and panic ensued. We activated all the DCI agents we had in the area to respond to the capitol. I listened on the radio as the Capitol Police and the few law enforcement officers still in the capitol kept falling back as they lost control of the floors to protestors. Ground floor, first floor, and then the second floor were being relinquished to the screaming throngs, and I recall thinking, "Keep them off the third floor!" because that is where the internal command post had been established early on.

I headed toward the capitol through the tunnel and emerged into the chaos. By this time, many people knew that I was law enforcement, and I always displayed my badge on my suit coat to make sure they knew I wasn't a legislator. I made my way through the crowd and finally got to the third floor by freight elevator where all the available law enforcement officers had sealed the top of each stairwell onto the floor, and we shut down the elevators. We could hardly communicate with each other as the noise levels reached deafening levels. I instructed all the DCI agents to wear their DOJ jackets and badges while positioning themselves with the uniformed officers. It was hours before things were under control again. You would think this would have been a valuable lesson in communicating objectives for the legislators, but that was not the mood or intention. This was political street fighting at its purest, and a surprise shiv to the chest in the process was not out of the realm of possibility. It was very sad.

On the day of the vote, the plan was to move the legislators onto city buses and away from the capitol to where their cars were being parked at the Alliant Energy Center. We began to quietly move our law enforcement staff into the area but were surprised to find that hundreds of protestors were already there. They were lined up several rows deep on the path from the capitol to where the buses would pull up. It was like they knew the plan.

When the buses pulled up, and the doors opened to get the legislators on board, the crowds erupted and surrounded the buses. They began rocking the buses back and forth, screaming and chanting. Eventually, law enforcement got the buses clear and they pulled away. But that was a spectacle we would have to avoid the next time around.

I was back in the governor's office early that next morning as our DCI tactical team calmly went over the protection-support details amidst the growing throng of protestors and chants. The law enforcement executive group, having been notified the night before that the bill would go to the assembly that day, wasted no time in planning for the eruption of protests we expected. I was in the governor's office with the governor, Mike Huebsch, Keith Gilkes, Eric Schutt, and some of their top aides. The governor's office felt we needed more manpower, even though we already had several hundred officers on site.

I called Milwaukee Police Chief Ed Flynn's office, and they told me he was unavailable, but they would give him the message I called. I waited for half an hour and called his cell phone. His voice told me he was aggravated by my call, as I told him that we needed more manpower, and we were requesting assistance under the Emergency Police Services mutual aid agreement. He responded, "Yesterday, I had to send my people over to get *your* governor out of the state office building where they were protesting him. I'm not inclined to send additional assistance for this." I reminded him this was not a political request but a public safety request, and he was unmoved. He refused to send more help.

"So much for the law enforcement brotherhood," I thought as I hung up the phone and announced his decision. Politics had once again interjected itself into what should have been a reasonable public safety response. It made me wonder what the fallout would be for Milwaukee in the wake of that decision by Chief Flynn.

With all this drama playing out, Keith Gilkes and Mike Huebsch called me aside. They wanted to know if I could arrange safe extraction of the Republican legislators immediately following the assembly vote. There was much concern over last night's attempt to manage the exit of the legislators with the city buses. I told them that we could do it, but I needed broad latitude. With their concerns over leaked information, we could not share information with the rest of the law enforcement executive group without compromising the objective. They agreed, and I met with my deputy administrator, Dave Matthews, to plan out the exfiltration.

We then met with the entire law enforcement executive group to discuss the assembly vote later that day. It was decided that they would execute the removal the same way as the night before with the city buses.

Matthews and I had met privately with Huebsch and told him of the actual plan we would execute. I told him we would need several 15-passenger vans from the Department of Administration to be quietly brought into the lowest level of the DOJ parking structure throughout the morning in staggered arrivals so as not to attract attention. After the vote, we would take the legislators down a stairway near their chambers to the lowest level of the capitol and then through the tunnel that connected it to the DOJ. Then, we would put them into these vans—not the city buses. Once the vans were full, we would quickly block traffic on Doty Street, and the vans would emerge and make their way to the Alliant Energy Center.

As the vote was about to be taken, I was in the assembly chambers. As predicted, the protestors started moving toward the bus staging area and surrounded the buses before the vote was even taken. They knew what those buses were there for. After the vote, the legislators made it quickly through the tunnel and into the waiting vans. As they pulled out and away, a single protestor standing near Martin Luther King Jr. Boulevard and Doty Street started screaming, "There they go! They're escaping!" And escape they did; it all went according to plan.

The plan went off without a hitch. For those that thought I was running my own "secret police" for the governor's office, I quietly pointed out that the DCI is tasked by law with investigations or actions at the request of the legislature or the governor, and no other law enforcement agency had that responsibility. This was their request and therefore our responsibility.

In the years that followed the Act 10 protests, Walker would disclose that his one "regret" was that his administration and the republicans didn't take more time to explain their intent and get the public's support before pushing the legislation through. Although I agree that a responsible governor and legislature would have done precisely that, I don't believe that would have ever been their intention. This appeared to be Walker trying to look responsible as an afterthought. But the reality was that we had a newly minted Republican majority with the governor, attorney general, and both houses. They were hell-bent to do something "big and bold," as the governor often called it. They wanted to demonstrate that they could do whatever they wanted, Democrats be damned. It was time to settle scores after eight years of Democratic leadership, and they would not waste time in doing so.

The governor signed the portion of the Act 10 law dealing with organized labor on Friday, March 11, 2011, and the wayward legislators returned the following day to the thunderous approval of the tens of thousands of protestors.

I was working out of the attorney general's office at the capitol that day and was used to the constant chanting in the outer vestibule. As the time approached to sign the bill, I made my way to the back of the

THE ACT 10 BOMBSHELL

governor's conference room, behind the gaggle of press. Aides moved to close the blinds so that the protestors outside would not be visible to the cameras. As with many things in politics, it's all about the window dressing, or obscuring in this case. Key Republicans streamed in to take their place behind the governor's signing desk, and they were all grinning like a butcher's dog. There were lots of congratulations and backslapping as they shook hands and waited for the governor to sweep in and sign the death knell to public sector unionization.

The screaming and chanting in the outer vestibule grew to a thunderous level as the moment for the signing approached. Even with the heavy outer doors to the entryway and the conference room doors closed, the roar was impressive. As I stood there, I wondered how many of those standing in the front of the room now would have done it differently if they could. They counted on some pushback, but they could not have possibly counted on what they got.

I had worked 32 straight days without a day off throughout the height of the protests. Finally, on a Sunday, I was going to stay home and catch up with the mountain of chores that were building up around the house. As I was trying to sleep in, I felt a little nudge on my arm and opened one eye to see my youngest daughter, Emily, standing next to the bed. She was smiling and said, "Dad, Mom said you might be able to take us down to the capitol to see the protests and walk through the underground tunnel." So much for my day off! I knew it would be a chance for the kids to see something they would likely never see again, so I acquiesced and got dressed.

We went down to DOJ headquarters, and I took the kids through the tunnel and into the capitol. From there we went out into the street and walked around the capitol with the marchers. Many cops and some of my own staff saw me walking with the kids and found it amusing, as I just gave them a smile and a nod to avoid slowing down the parade. I explained to the kids that this was what democracy looked like. That chant still echoes in my head. ❧

BECOMING SECRETARY OF CORRECTIONS

Over the next year and a half, life began to settle down some. We were still busy in the DCI with the multitude of background investigations for all the governor's appointments, and our criminal caseload was expanding. We had to meet with Transition Director John Hiller and ask him to stop sending multiple prospective candidates for every position because it took too much time. At one point, we had nearly half of the division working on background investigations. We asked that they narrow down the possibilities to a couple of people per position, and we would get them those results. Eventually, at the request of the governor's office, we created a modified and shortened background investigation package that hit the main points but did not go into the detail we normally would have done.

Some of the information revealed in those backgrounds prevented some candidates from being appointed to positions. We would make the recommendation to the transition team, and they would decide on the appointment. In some cases, they disregarded our recommendations, but we didn't take that personally. We could only advise, and they would decide.

Since Gary Hamblin had been the administrator of the DOJ Division of Law Enforcement Services before being selected to become secretary of the DOC, that meant that his old DOJ administrator position was open. It was a political appointment for Attorney General J.B. Van Hollen to fill, and J.B. asked me if I had any recommendations for it. He wanted it to go to someone with a law enforcement background. Without hesitation, I said, "Brian O'Keefe." Brian was a retired deputy chief from the Milwaukee Police Department, and I had worked with him on many cases and grant programs in the past. He was excellent at managing budgets and grant programs as well as working closely with law enforcement.

I had spoken with Brian just a few weeks before, and he said he was looking to leave his retirement job with BMO Harris Bank in Milwaukee, where he was involved in corporate security. J.B. asked me to have lunch with Brian and see if he was interested, which I did. Brian said he would absolutely like the job, and I told him I would be in touch. After delivering the information to J.B., he asked me to set up a meeting with himself and Brian. J.B. met with Brian, and subsequently Brian got the political appointment.

When Brian came to the DOJ, he did very well. We worked closely together and served on many of the same law enforcement executive boards together. Brian could be rough around the edges and seemed to want to intimidate people at times. More than a few people considered him a bit of a bully, but my personal feeling was it was just Milwaukee Police bravado, and it never slowed me down.

One day in June 2012, my assistant advised me that the governor's new chief of staff, Eric Schutt, was going to come over to see me and have his official photo taken by our photographer with the state flags in the background. I had met Eric for lunch after he became chief of staff and found him to be exceptional. He was personable, quick-witted, and did not waste time with nonsense.

When Eric arrived, he came into my office and closed the door. He looked at my credenza and saw the picture there of my wife and me with the governor and another of us with the Van Hollens at the inauguration.

He said, "That's a nice picture of you guys," to which I agreed. Without missing a beat, he said, "The governor wants to know if you will be the secretary of the DOC." I had only been off my probation as the DCI administrator a matter of weeks, and he apparently knew that since I had turned this position down once before due to my probationary period.

I looked down and said, "Why me?" And he said that I was widely respected by law enforcement across the state, and they *needed* me to go to the DOC and take control.

Eric went on to share that Gary Hamblin had been talking about leaving soon, and they wanted someone lined up who they knew could handle the job. I told him that I needed the weekend to discuss it with my family, and I would get back to him the following Monday. My head was spinning. Corrections? Cabinet secretary? That agency is huge and has a reputation for being a cauldron of discontent. They also had the most organized and vocal union in the state, and they were undoubtedly still reeling from the Act 10 bombshell. Why would anyone want that job?

I went upstairs and spoke with Bonnie Cyganek, the administrator of Management Services for the DOJ. Taking her into my confidence, I told her I needed to weigh the options of this possible appointment but would not take the position if I was not guaranteed restoration to my position as DCI administrator. Bonnie was very excited and said she would get back to me, and I went back to my office with my head still swimming. All the way down, I kept thinking, "Don't do this. Stay where you are. Politicians are dangerous." But common sense would not take hold. It was a dizzying realization that I was being asked to take over an agency with over 10,000 employees—the sixth largest employer in the state—with an enormous budget and even more enormous responsibilities.

Bonnie came down to my office a short time later and advised me that the law guaranteed my restoration to the DCI administrator position because it was a civil service position and there were no comparable jobs in state government. She directed me to Department of Administration Memo MRS-211 that detailed my restoration rights and further advised that the elevated salary would also go toward my highest years' earnings for my retirement. It would be a significant amount if I stayed three years. The DOJ director of human resources also confirmed Bonnie's information.

Next, I called to speak with former Deputy Attorney General Ray Taffora, who had left at the beginning of J.B.'s second term. Ray was surprised but seemed impressed. I told him that I was not inclined to take the position because I loved my job as DCI administrator. Ray had great experience with political operations, having served under Tommy Thompson, and his advice meant a lot to me. I asked him to tell me how to say no to the offer. In typical Ray fashion, he paused and said, "Edward, let me get this straight. You, as a non-politician, are being asked by the governor with arguably the highest-priced political stock in the country to run his largest cabinet agency with the largest budget. Why don't you tell me how you say no to that?" He then said, "Edward, when you have the governor calling you, asking you to lead, that is a call you need to take."

"Thanks, Ray," I said. "That isn't the answer I was looking for." And we both just laughed. After that, I had to speak with J.B., so I drove to a hotel in Appleton where he was attending a conference. We went and sat in the restaurant area, and I told him about the offer. He was surprised but recognized it for what it was. He told me, "I don't want to lose you. But how many people will ever have the opportunity to lead an agency that big? Imagine what that position would be in the private sector!" He then thought for a moment and said, "If I wasn't doing this job, and I was offered that, I would take it." He gave his blessing reluctantly, as Jim Doyle had given his blessing once before for my career move back to the DCI.

When I got home that night, my wife and I sat with our kids, and we discussed the opportunity. Just realizing that I needed to look at it as an opportunity as opposed to a detriment was a big step forward.

Ultimately, the family agreed that this was a unique chance to lead, and they gave their stamp of approval. Three sleepless nights later, I came into the office and called Eric to tell him I would accept the position if I was guaranteed restoration to my DCI position. Eric said that my restoration to that position was guaranteed by law. He then said that the appointment might take some time because Gary had not submitted his resignation yet, and they didn't want to push him. He asked that I keep the appointment quiet. I wish he had told me that at the outset! I went back to the few people I had spoken to and asked them to please keep it under wraps, which they did.

Weeks went by, and I was focused on DCI work but quietly learning about the DOC by reading the department annual reports, institution annual reports, news articles, organizational charts, policy manuals, and anything else I could find online. Then, in the beginning of October, Mike Huebsch called and told me he was sending over one of his budget analysts who handled the DOC to brief me. She called me, and we set up an appointment to be held in my conference room at the DCI.

My assistant, Dawn, who had arranged the meeting, asked why a DOA budget analyst would be coming over to meet with me. I told her it was regarding some other state business I was involved in. When the analyst arrived, she was pulling a small handcart with boxes of documents behind her. Dawn showed her into the conference room, and I went to join her. As she was closing the door, with Dawn standing nearby, she said, "Mr. Secretary, this is not going to be like any budget briefing you have ever had." I looked at Dawn through the window as the door closed, and her eyes were wide. I put my finger to my lips and mouthed, "Shh," and the analyst and I sat down for the two-hour briefing.

It was staggering to learn the amount of money that the DOC had budgeted. The biennial budget was about $2.65 billion. Numbers were flashing in front of me as all the various accounts were summarized. Roughly, I calculated in my head, that was about $110 million a month or $3.6 million a day over a biennium. Oh, my Lord! My DCI budget was about $18 million a year. I asked how I was expected to manage that size budget, and she said not to worry; the budget shop at DOC was great. I wish that made me feel better.

The next day, Eric Schutt called me and said the governor wanted to meet with me. I went across the street and met with the governor, Eric, and Mike Huebsch. The governor welcomed me, and I found him affable as always. We sat across the table from each other, and he asked if I would accept his appointment as secretary of the DOC. I said I would, provided I was guaranteed restoration back to my DCI position. I had told the governor that I tried to stay away from politics, and this was somewhat of an uncomfortable position for me. He put my mind at ease. He told me that he just expected me to run my department, and he preferred that I stayed away from politics. I told him that I did not give money to politicians, and I wouldn't be giving any to him either. He just smiled and said that was how he wanted it. In fact, he said he wanted none of his cabinet giving money to campaigns. That made me feel better. Maybe I could work below the political fray and just make positive changes. I would learn that I had a better chance of sprouting wings and flying away.

We discussed some of the challenges ahead for me with the DOC. There was the issue of escalating populations of geriatric prisoners, union discord, cost-saving efficiencies he wanted me to look for, and of course, the budget. However, there was no mention of concerns that had been raised to him by a judge in Racine County ten months before I came into office involving problems at the state's juvenile detention facilities, Lincoln Hills and Copper Lake Schools. Three and a half years later, in February 2016, as I was leaving my position because of those problems, those judge's concerns would surface in the media. I was just as surprised as everyone else when I read it in the paper. Who decided to sweep that little tidbit under the rug? Why wasn't I advised? Because if I had been, I would have taken action on day one to start addressing it.

As we left the governor's office and went into Eric's office, he and Mike congratulated me with smiles and firm handshakes saying,

"Congratulations, Mr. Secretary." It sounded so strange to hear. They told me the press release would go out in the next few days, and they needed to let Gary Hamblin know.

Gary and I went to breakfast a couple of days later and had a pleasant conversation on what was ahead of me. He had done a great job getting the DOC through the Act 10 bombshell without too many problems, which was monumental. However, one comment he made to me would never leave my memory: "There's always a crisis in Corrections." Boy, was he right!

As I prepared to depart for my new leadership position, my heart was still tied to the DCI. It was a bittersweet feeling, but I had been guaranteed by state law, state policy, and representations by the governor's office and DOJ that I would be welcomed back at the end of my service in the cabinet. It was only because of those guarantees that I was leaving.

J.B. and I met several times concerning who he would put in my place while I was on leave of absence. Brian O'Keefe wanted the position badly and was doing everything he could to get it. Brian was a friend and a good man, but he already had the opportunity to finish his career once with the Milwaukee Police Department and was now in his retirement job as a political appointee, which I had arranged for him.

I felt that for continuity in leadership, J.B. would be better off moving my deputy administrator, Dave Matthews, into that role. Dave had expressed his desire for the job, and I thought he would continue with my path in leading a very talented agency of criminal investigators. Dave also understood that I had restoration rights back to my position and would be able to pivot back to deputy when the time came for my return. I knew Brian would not see it that way. Ultimately, J.B. went with my recommendation and chose Dave for the position. J.B. would announce the decision at the upcoming DCI inservice, which would be my last appearance with the entire division before leaving for the DOC.

At my going-away get-together at the DOJ, the room was packed with well-wishers. There were laudatory and laughable comments made by the leadership and some gifts that various people had brought along. Most of them were funny reminders of my years of work with the agency. However, Brian could not hide his simmering animosity over my support for Dave as the new DCI administrator. You could see it in his eyes. When it came time for gifts, Brian gave me a gift-wrapped rat trap that I opened in front of the crowd. He said it was for the DOC budget staff to keep me away from the money, but I knew exactly what the intent was behind the rat trap. Brian felt that I had betrayed him by doing what I thought was right for the agency. That "gift" was similar to a mafia message, like receiving a dead fish wrapped in a newspaper. I would never have guessed where that would lead in the next few years to come. ♦

8

TAKING THE REINS

Before I left the DCI, I knew I would have to select my DOC leadership team. I would need a deputy secretary, an assistant deputy secretary, and I would be able to replace the four division administrators, as they were direct appointments by the secretary. There were other positions that I could also change, but they weren't critical in the early going. Eric Schutt had told me that I could pick my team and gave no requirements that they would be overseeing my selections. In other words, they wouldn't be handing me politically connected people who needed a job.

Now I could do what many secretaries have done in the past and bring in friends or others who I had personal or work relationships with, but that was not my style. The DOC was obviously a huge beast to try and get my arms around, and the last thing I needed was another person who didn't know how the agency operated. I needed someone to turn on the lights, not wander in the dark with me.

When I was the DCI administrator, I had won the charity auction for firewood supplied by the DOC and Oakhill Correctional Institution. I went over one day with a truck and trailer to pick up my wood and had to stop at the front of the building to have someone take me to the wood. After identifying myself, I went down to the firewood area. I was there just a few minutes when a state car pulled up, and out stepped Deirdre "Dede" Morgan. Dede was the warden of Oakhill Correctional Institution, and we had met not that long before at the attorney general's conference. She struck me immediately as a go-getter, and she again displayed that same enthusiasm when we met at the woodpile as the inmates began loading my trailer.

Dede asked if I had ever seen Oakhill before. I told her I hadn't. She invited me for a quick tour while the inmates worked. Throughout my tour, I was again impressed with her unbridled enthusiasm for what she did and the mission of her agency. She made corrections sound exciting. I was also impressed that she knew every officer by name and even knew many of the inmates by name. Dede just flowed from one building to the next and made it all look so easy. Her knowledge of corrections was obviously deep. She had been the parole commission chair, served as the assistant deputy secretary under a former secretary, and worked in all four of the agency's divisions. I left that day with my firewood, still impressed with the warden I had spent the last hour with. Neither of us realized at that moment that our time together that day had essentially been an interview for a position down the road as my deputy secretary

When I was asked to take the position as secretary and told I could pick my team, I didn't have a moment's hesitation in deciding who my choice would be for deputy secretary. The question was, "Who would accept the position and the task of babysitting a corrections neophyte?" To this day, I count my lucky stars she said yes. Over the coming years, Dede would become my closest confidant and one of my best friends. She would understand what a handful I could be and learned how to manage me almost as well as my wife, who she also became very close with. They say that behind every successful man is a great woman, but in my case, there were two. I was blessed.

In the short term, I kept Gary Hamblin's assistant deputy in place to help with continuity. He would eventually leave for a position in another agency, and I brought in Brigadier General Scott Legwold, who was retiring from his military career to serve as assistant deputy secretary. Scott was an outstanding logistics manager and had proven himself through years of service with the Armed Forces and National Guard. The DOC had over 1,100 active duty, reserve, or retired military members. Unfortunately, we also had over 1,000 former military members as inmates, but they still deserved respect for their service despite what led them to prison. I always appreciated the way military members approached their jobs: dedication, team, mission, plan, and execute. These were all the qualities that Scott would bring to the table.

When I first arrived at the DOC, it was beyond intimidating. Walking up to that huge building, I thought to myself, "Are you sure you are ready for this?" When I walked inside and saw the wall of former DOC secretary pictures and my picture next to the governor's, it stopped me in my tracks. I wondered what legacies they had left behind them. What were the times like when they took control of this enormous agency? What were their greatest challenges? What would be mine? How can you please such a diverse population of inmates and staff? I would learn soon enough—you could not.

My secretary's office was expansive. It was large enough for my large desk, a couch, a couple of guest chairs, and a conference table that seated six. There was also a private bathroom, which was a nice amenity. All of this was because the state was leasing the former American Family Insurance national headquarters, not because the state built it this way. My office was the American Family president's office back in the day, and the DOC secretary was the lucky tenant.

My assistant, Cheryl, was the picture of efficiency. She had a cheerful disposition, and she seemed to effortlessly handle the logistics involved with the secretary's position. It took a few weeks before I realized exactly how much that job entailed. She was patient with the newest leader in a revolving door of appointees and walked me through the changes my life would see. Essentially, you will need to learn on the fly and best of luck.

As secretary, you never owned your schedule. Multiple people would have access to it, each one thinking that their concern was more important. I could expect to be called without warning to "meet and greets" throughout the building for groups or VIP visitors in any of the four divisions.

Travel arrangements would be handled by Cheryl or another assistant. Cheryl explained that I would need to delegate responses to inquiries or action requests to others. Don't read the mail, because most of it would be complaints or lawsuits. Yes, you will be sued, a lot—more than any other cabinet official. Be prepared for press attention, most of it bad. Don't speak with the press; have your public affairs people handle that. Legislators will want to talk with you; make sure your responses are coordinated with the governor's office. You will be invited or expected at various official functions, such as the State of the State, budget address, and executive residence receptions. You will serve as a surrogate for the governor at various functions such as funerals, ribbon cuttings, public stakeholder meetings, and events at the capitol. Remember, your job is to support the administration and not your own agenda.

The governor's cabinet meetings will be every other week. One will be with secretaries and their staff in the governor's conference room, and the other will be dinner at the executive residence with only the secretaries. You are expected to attend and bring your deputy secretary or assistant deputy secretary to the staff inclusive meeting. Be prepared for discussions on any issues the DOC is involved with, and have a working knowledge of budget issues at all times. Be prepared to travel to the capitol at a moment's notice or answer questions from the governor's office on the fly. If you don't know the answers, know who does have the answers. Get ready because your life does not slow down; it speeds up.

Throughout my career, serving in different leadership positions, I would grow more amused with each advancement on how wrong my impression of leadership had been. There was not more time off; in fact, there was much less time off. Life was not a string of cocktail parties on yachts or meetings on golf courses. In the end, it is your family that pays the highest price for your public service as you become a ghost who is occasionally seen. And often times, when you were at home, you were exhausted by constant 12-to 14-hour days.

People would move into your orbit and try to get close to the flagpole. Your power and authority reflected on them like the glow of a candle if they stood close enough. Often, they worked to break through the acquaintance label and into the friend category by flattering you or by handling some mundane or unpleasant task of yours, quietly wiggling through a crease in your protective armor to obtain an affiliation they hoped would translate into their own perceived power or status. However, when things went bad, they would evaporate like early morning fog on a sunny day.

I had met with each of the division administrators for the DOC individually before I came for my first day. They had all been appointed by Gary Hamblin before me and understood that their positions were "at will," and I could replace them. However, I asked each one of them to stay in their positions. These were four seasoned corrections professionals with decades of experience. They knew how to run their operations and understood their roles. Professionals in the DOC management ranks are well versed in turning on a dime as leadership changed, because it frequently did. These were four eminently qualified women who had risen to these levels in a profession that was once dominated by men. They were serious, smart, and focused, and I knew I needed them with me in steering this ship. I was grateful they agreed to stay on.

When I came into my first executive staff meeting in the secretary's conference room, there were about 20 people present, and everyone was standing behind their chairs. I stopped and looked around, asking "Why are you folks all standing?" I was advised they were waiting for me before they took their seats. I just laughed and said, "Have a seat. That's not necessary with me. You'll find I'm a lot more laid back than that!" I could see it would be a challenge getting these crisp professionals to loosen up.

One of the first things that we did in my administration, at my deputy secretary's urging, was to convene a breakfast for all the former corrections secretaries. All except Gary Hamblin could make it, and it was an eye-opening experience. These men all shared the same challenges I was now embarking on, and each had his own outlook on the agency, the role of the secretary, and the biggest headaches ahead. Their insight into union issues, staff challenges, political interaction, and relationships with the governors they served was very interesting and diverse. It was an excellent meeting and the first time anything like that had ever been done by a cabinet secretary. It was brilliant, but all the credit went to Dede Morgan. She would prove time and again that she was smarter than a tree full of owls, and I relied on her to keep me from walking off cliffs.

Dede and I made a great team. We both led with our hearts, gave every effort we could, and strived to humanize an agency that had been maligned by the press and politicians for years. In my first week, I wrote an email to all the staff in the DOC introducing myself and some of my basic principles. Just after I hit "send," Dede swept into my office and said, "Are you crazy? These people are going to respond, and they won't all be nice." Over 10,000 employees were going to have a chance to scream at the mountain. I told Dede that was fine with me because I wanted a barometer of the mindset, and I would answer every one of them myself. She just smiled and said, "Okay, you're the secretary."

In less than an hour, there were over 400 replies, as my email alert chime kept reminding me that people had something to say. And that number would grow with every shift change as we headed into the weekend. I spent most of the weekend responding to every single email, as I would for the rest of my DOC career, personally responding to thousands of emails from staff. Most were very polite and nice, some not so much, and a couple were pretty bad. I kept in mind that our staff had been through a traumatic upheaval with Act 10 and sat down in my recliner to read and respond to the notes. It was Saturday morning, and my wife joined me in the living room with her coffee.

I read her a few of the notes, and then I stopped short and read this one aloud: "Dear Secretary Wall. You are a piece of shit. You were appointed by that piece of shit Scott Walker and will try to hurt the DOC. Give us back our union rights."

It was signed by the officer and sent from his DOC email address. He obviously wasn't trying to hide his identity.

My wife's eyes went wide, and she was equally as surprised as I was. There was a lack of respect for the position and the governor, but beyond that, I noted there was no compunction in saying what he thought.

I replied to the officer, "Hi, I'm sorry you feel this way. We haven't even had a chance to meet, and hopefully, we can educate each other on what the needs of the department are going forward."

The reply came within minutes, "OMG, I didn't know anyone read these emails. Please forgive me and don't tell my warden." I could feel his tight sphincter muscles reverberating through my iPad and just chuckled.

To put him at ease, I replied, "LOL, I read everything. Now that we have moved past the introductions, maybe we could talk about how to improve the department."

We subsequently developed a pen pal relationship that would span my time at the DOC. You see, it was not that important that we agreed on everything. What was important was that he and the other 10,000-plus employees knew that they could talk to the guy in charge and he would answer them. Maybe not with the answer they wanted, but they would hear something, and that was important. In three and a half years I answered thousands of emails from staff, not because I wanted to but because they deserved it.

Early on, I embarked on a statewide road show to visit as many of the institutions and offices as I could in a couple of weeks' time. Many of these would be short stops for a chance to say hello to staff and management. I wanted to get a face-to-face pulse from the people I'd be working with. I knew there was much anger and resentment over Act 10, and the DOC was the hardest hit of any state agency. It was also the agency with one of the most militant labor unions.

On one of my first institution visits, I was greeted in the parking lot by an officer who was very polite and squared away. He held the door for me and escorted me to the superintendent's office. He was a nice guy and seemed happy. Two weeks later, he committed suicide by hanging himself. When they called to let me know what had happened, I was stunned. Like every other case of suicide that I had ever dealt with, I wondered what we could have done as an agency to help prevent it. Was there a cry for help? Were there signs of what was coming? These were the same questions I would ask five more times during my three and a half years at the helm of the DOC.

When I arrived at the officer's funeral, it was far different than I expected. Cop funerals always were packed with representatives of the brotherhood from far and wide. That was not the case with corrections. I was surprised at how few people showed up from the DOC, and they were equally surprised that I was there. One officer walked up and asked me, "Mr. Secretary, what are you doing here?" I was taken aback by the question as if they expected I wouldn't be there.

"We lost one of our own," I said. "Of course, I would be here." He just looked at me with a blank stare and shrugged, walking away without a word. I wondered what kind of world I had wandered into.

A few months later, I was called at home one night by Dede. She advised me that another officer had attempted suicide by hanging and was being med-flighted to Madison. I headed straight to the hospital and got there shortly after the helicopter. Dede arrived shortly thereafter, as it was both of our instincts to just go and be there and help.

I was advised that the officer's parents lived in the Upper Peninsula of Michigan and were driving down. They would arrive in about five hours. I asked if I could stay with him, as he was alone on a respirator in the intensive care unit. They asked if I was family and I simply said, "No, I work with him. He should have someone at his side to know we are here." The nurse then asked what work I did with the officer, and I replied, "I'm just a secretary," and she said it would be okay. She walked me into the room, and I sat down beside the officer and took his hand in mine. His eyes opened, and he turned his head to look at me with questioning eyes. I could tell he didn't know who I was, and I told him to just relax, that I was going to stay with him. He still had the confused look on his face, as if he was saying, "Who are you?"

I just said, "I work at headquarters. My name is Ed Wall." His eyes opened wide. He knew the name, and I urged him to relax and know that we were with him and his parents were on their way. For the next six hours, Dede and I took turns holding his hand and just talking. In that room, with medical apparatus all around and the rhythm of the respirator, there was a feeling of loneliness that crept over me as the hours went by. We were the only people from the DOC who showed up.

When his parents arrived at about 4:00 a.m., Dede and I met with them and explained what we knew. His mother just cried quietly while his father kept staring at his son. I knew what they were thinking. How? Why? What could we have done? What will we do? They were lucky because they would eventually have some answers and be able to move forward. That officer went on to make a full recovery and eventually returned to work months later. When he returned, I traveled up to his institution and met with him privately. It was nice to see him standing and talking. He had one question for me: Why had I come to be with him at the hospital?

I simply said, "That's my job—to be there." Life would go on for him, and for that I was thankful.

After leaving the hospital and with just a couple hours of sleep, I asked Dede to set up a conference call with all the wardens and superintendents across the state. As they all called in, I waited patiently for the roll call to be completed. When everyone was confirmed in attendance, I related the story of the officer's attempted suicide the night before and the fact that nobody from the DOC aside from me and the deputy secretary showed up at the hospital. After letting that sink in for a moment, I followed up with this caution: "Our job is to be there to support our staff, in good times and bad. If we have a future attempted suicide or critical incident involving one of our staff members that requires them to be admitted to the hospital, God help the warden or superintendent who doesn't show up, and you better beat me there, because I'm coming." I went on to calmly explain that if our command staff felt that they did not have a duty to the staff who worked for them, then we would find a position for them that did not require that kind of commitment. I never beat a warden or superintendent to the hospital after that day.

This was an unusual tack for me to take because I am not inclined to bravado or bullish action. My temperament is more suited to discussion and reasoning, but in this case, my emotions carried the moment. I was still incredulous at the thought that leaders would not be moved to stand by the side of their people when they were critically hurt, regardless of how they got hurt.

The stigma surrounding suicide became obvious as my time at the DOC would go on, and that spilled over into the way staff and management alike would respond to it. Having my friend and supervisor, Craig Klyve, commit suicide changed me forever. I didn't understand why it happened and could not comprehend why someone would consider a permanent solution to a temporary problem. However, I did know that it was a problem that our agency would have to confront head-on after being advised that we had nearly 40 suicides by staff over the last several years.

One of the programs I was proudest of starting within the DOC was the suicide awareness program, and we started classes to deal with it across the department. There was an unsettling fact that seemed to run through the five suicides we had while I was at the DOC. Some people saw it coming but didn't know how to take steps to intervene. The agency was blessed with staff who had personal and heartbreaking experience with suicide, and they would step forward to lead the efforts, and they will forever have my gratitude for their good works. They saved lives, and they would continue to save lives with those classes after my time with the agency was through.

In my mind, a legacy was about not what you did but the programs that would outlast you.

The DOC was a strange place to work in coming from the traditional law enforcement world. As my time would go on, I would try and reconcile the differences. In police work, we dealt with the problems of the world on a street level. We dealt with criminals for whatever time was required to either resolve an issue, get them into custody or sent to prison, and then we moved on. There was always another call to answer, another patrol to go on, another criminal to apprehend.

While the police dealt with these criminals for hours, the DOC dealt with them for years. As a cop, you understood that a small percentage of the people you dealt with were going to be dangerous criminals, and you had to be on your guard. For correctional officers, the reality was much different. One hundred percent of the people you would be tasked with overseeing were convicted felons—felons in some cases with nothing better to do than watch you and figure out how they would aggravate or even try to kill you. That kind of constant, daily pressure can build in the mind of the corrections officer, and the way you look at your surroundings can become toxic. You start to think that everyone is plotting against you—the inmates, your supervisors, or even your coworkers. And on the outside, the public doesn't appreciate you. The politicians took away your union, the only entity you were taught was there to protect you. Those same politicians also wouldn't give the agency meaningful funding, wouldn't recognize the danger of their jobs, and wouldn't invest money in improving the prison system.

From the outside, the DOC seems like a dark and dreary world, akin to a rainy *Batman* movie, with evil at every corner and lurking bad guys who are difficult to make out through the dim light. In some cases, that perception is not far from the truth, depending on which staff member you speak to. However, I found something much different when I came into my position, and I was surprised at how my outlook evolved by the end of my tenure.

TAKING THE REINS

In my first road tour of the institutions, I went to Waupun Correctional Institution, one of the state's maximum-security prisons, also known as "The Walls." The Walls was over 150 years old and the state's first prison. It is one of the oldest operating prisons in the country. Being a history fan, I was amazed at the story of its beginnings and the changes it saw in the years following. You can't help but be struck by how massive it is with its stone, steel bars, catwalks, and towers. It's everything you would picture a prison to look like from the 1800s. With that history comes a certain swagger that some of the officers and supervisors at The Walls had adopted over the decades. If you worked at The Walls, you were a different breed of officer; you were old school, and you did not take guff. You were tougher than the rest.

When I first walked through the cell houses at Waupun, I met with different staff and spoke to them openly. Many were respectful, some not so much. Yes, I was the secretary, but to many that just meant I was an extension of the man who had taken away their union rights and diminished their already meager income. There was a simmering anger and distrust that I would find almost everywhere I went. It did not take long to understand the sentiment, which caused my mind to wonder how I could possibly affect their situation in the face of a political action that had already divided the state so badly.

As I walked into one of the cell houses with my staff and the warden in tow, I was introduced to a seasoned sergeant. I asked him if I could walk with him down the length of the cell hall so I could speak with him. I motioned for my staff to stay behind, and we just walked slowly and talked. I shared with him that I was just a cop, not a politician, and was surprised by how divisive the atmosphere was. He just stopped and turned to me, saying, "Secretary, you don't get it. This didn't just start with Act 10; this has gone on for years, and it won't stop. Come work in here for a while, and you might understand. Prisons change both inmates and staff. Act 10 just made it worse."

Mulling over those honest words as we walked back toward the group of staff waiting patiently for us at the other end of the hall, I tried to figure out how I could help make the situation better. I feared there was no passion to serve or reason to have hope in our mission. The impacts of Act 10 on the average government worker were negative, but the impacts in a negative environment like the prisons only magnified the issues tenfold.

As we rejoined the entourage, around the corner came a towering officer, the kind of guy I would have wanted to go through the door on a search warrant with me in years past. I stuck my hand out, and he shook it, his huge hand engulfing mine. "Hello, sir," he said. I then noticed that he was carrying a can of crayons with some paper and following behind him was an obviously challenged inmate. I casually asked the officer what he was going to be doing, and he smiled and said, "We are going to work on making some Christmas cards for his family." He then led the inmate into a room with tables and began laying out the crayons.

I turned away as if looking back down the cell hall. My eyes started to tear up as I caught myself in another unfair characterization of the agency I was asked to lead. The contrast between rough, tough, unyielding officers who rule with an iron fist and the gentle giant leading an inmate in to help make Christmas cards was stunning. There were so many facets of this agency that the public would never understand. They were not just places of punishment and deprivation; there was compassion, caring, and understanding beneath the ironclad exterior. There was hope.

In another early stop at Taycheedah, the women's prison, I went into one of the oldest inmate buildings on the grounds. There in the middle of the day room was a large table with a bunch of elderly women sitting around it making quilts. There were quilts stacked on tables and chairs around the room, and I walked over to introduce myself. It was all so surreal, these little old ladies chatting and working as if they were at a church social.

When I walked up, one lady who was closest to me smiled and said hello. I was taken aback as she looked and sounded so much like my own grandmother. She introduced herself and the other ladies around the table. Then she explained that they were making quilts for children in the hospital and the homeless. I recall thinking that this was a wonderful program that gave back so much to the communities.

As I was leaving, I stopped to talk with the seasoned female sergeant who was overseeing the day room. I told her how impactful my visit was and how much the little old lady I had spoken with reminded me of my grandmother. The sergeant just looked at me and asked very matter-of-factly, "Did your grandmother murder your grandfather, cut off his head, hands, and feet, and bury him the backyard?" My mouth fell open, and I just answered, "No," and she replied, "Then she's not really that much like your grandmother." She went on to explain that most of the women in that housing unit were serving life sentences, primarily for one-time "act of passion" murders. They would never leave.

That's how I started going down a path in my mind that convinced me the DOC was far more than it appeared. Programs for inmates, counseling and treatment, acts of kindness and compassion by staff and inmates alike were all part of the DOC. Unfortunately, the public only saw the union fights and the problems that made the press. I could not understand why the good things about corrections did not garner any attention or praise, but as I would find out, politics was at the core.

As a new secretary, I was introduced to the Association of State Correctional Administrators (ASCA), which was comprised of all the state corrections agency heads in the United States, Puerto Rico, and Guam. ASCA is an elite fraternity of people who know what you are dealing with as a DOC secretary and the cost of political decisions they have little control over. When I was introduced to ASCA, I was beyond impressed. These were men and women in the same position I was, trying to bring calm to chaos while still being able to live with their decisions. This was a group that I knew I would appreciate and rely on.

In the first few months of my administration, I attended "new secretary school" that was run by ASCA. During that time, we were engaged at several different levels with other experienced secretaries and directors from across the country. I had specifically asked to be paired with Tom Clements, the executive director of the Colorado Department of Corrections, so that I could pick his brain about their outstanding prison industries programs. Tom was a very easygoing man with exceptional experience, having been in the corrections world for over 30 years.

When Tom and I got to talk, I asked him many questions about prison industries, and he was patient in answering. However, Tom took the time to teach me what the real concern should be in the corrections world, and it was not one I had given much thought to. As I would learn through those few days we had together, the "somebody else's problem" attitude I had as a cop was now my problem, and we had a duty as corrections leaders to create better answers than we had been using.

In the business of corrections, you always had to weigh the risks of everything. Staff safety was paramount, as was the custody and care of people that society found too dangerous to be walking amongst us. There were tools at the disposal of those in the prisons to deal with the violent, uncooperative, noncompliant, or endangered inmates. "Segregation" was one of the tools frequently used. Often referred to as "solitary confinement" by those opposed to it, I found this tool had a propensity to be overused. Indeed, there were many cases where inmates would be in segregation for years on end, albeit sometimes out of necessity. The damage that this isolation and sensory deprivation can do to the mind was immense. Tom Clements was a leader in trying to effect changes in the use of segregation, and he understood that in many cases we were actually making already dangerous people exponentially more dangerous.

Not long after new secretary school, I was back in Wisconsin trying to figure out how to bring all my newfound knowledge and understanding to the DOC. It was March 17, 2013, when I received the call that Tom had been shot and killed at his front door, in the presence of his family, by an inmate who had been released from prison a short time before. That inmate had been confined in segregation for seven years and was released directly into the public. The circumstances behind the murder of Tom Clements have not been fully unraveled, but the one fact that struck all of us was the inmate's confinement in segregation for such an extended period. The very practice Tom had been advocating against found its way to his doorstep and took his life.

Segregation reform became a very big issue in corrections agencies across the country, and I would join that chorus calling for dramatic changes. At the next cabinet meeting, I voiced my concerns about segregation reform and related the story of Tom Clements and what he had taught me, both through his life and his death. The other secretaries shook their heads at the real-life drama that swirled around corrections and the secretary's personal risk in doing the job. The governor looked at me while I was talking, his head nodding as it usually did when someone else was speaking. However, I recall that as I looked at him while speaking, his eyes were devoid of feeling or warmth. The eyes are the window to the soul, and his eyes were not in agreement with the political nods he was giving for the crowd. They were cold, and I felt as I spoke that he did not agree with my conclusions.

My embracing the cause of segregation reform was not as warmly greeted by the Walker administration as I had hoped. In context, I was working for the governor who authored the tough-on-crime bills in the 1990s, which turned out to be the driving force in our exploding prison population. The population of inmates over 60 years old was escalating dramatically, and we would spend much of my term trying to get funding to accommodate a growing geriatric population. By the time I left, we had over 1,000 inmates that were 60 years old or older. Inmates have a physiological age typically 10 years above their numeric age due to the prison lifestyle. The unfortunate reality was that we would need to build a geriatric prison if the problems with "truth in sentencing" could not be addressed through legislation.

Many people have their visions of what prison is or should be, and that typically can be traced back to their upbringing and their religious or political beliefs. With that, the first time you walk into a cell hall filled with geriatric inmates, it causes you to reflect. Men sitting in wheelchairs, crawling along with walkers, or propped up in a chair unable to care for themselves are not the vision most would have. However, they are the reality of life sentences, and those inmates cost the taxpayers a fortune to take care of.

During my tenure as secretary, we had so many good stories to tell. Unfortunately, as our governor gazed longingly toward the White House, the level of micromanagement would ratchet up significantly. For example, the inmates at Red Granite Correctional Institution had done an incredible job refurbishing the wheelchairs for the Honor Flight Network for veterans. They worked very hard, and I checked in on them a few times in my travels around the state to see their progress. When they were all done, and the wheelchairs were looking beautiful, I called Jocelyn Webster, the governor's director of communications, and let her know what we had accomplished and that we would like to do a positive story on it with the press.

Jocelyn was a contrast in personalities. At times, she was pleasant; at other times, she was impossible to work with. Her temperament was a distraction to many of the cabinet secretaries, and we made that clear to the chief of staff, who at that time was Rich Zipperer, a former politician himself. When I asked Jocelyn to allow us to go with the wheelchair story, which was also during Walker's failed presidential bid, she said, "The only way you will run that story is if the governor is standing there loading those wheelchairs into the back of the truck himself, and he won't be doing that. You don't understand, Ed. Nothing good comes out of Corrections." Those words would ring in my ears for the remainder of my tenure: "Nothing good comes out of Corrections."

The governor happened to attend one of my early cabinet meetings, which was not that frequent as I would learn going forward. We had a few minutes to chat, and he asked, "How are things with the inmates at DOC?"

I pulled my head back and replied, "The inmates? If all I had to do was worry about the inmates, I could be playing golf three days a week. Most of my time is spent dealing with staff issues, budget problems, and crisis management." He just smiled and patted me on the shoulder, moving along to say hello to the next secretary. That interaction was instructive of how the administration would look at the DOC. Ten seconds to say hello, a pat on the shoulder, and on to something else. Nothing to see here. Move along.

As my time with the DOC went on, I would discover that within the chest of this tough and rugged agency beat a heart dedicated to the service of others. Even the inmates worked to create a variety of arts and crafts that would be donated to charities for auctions. One of the changes I made early on, to save the state money and give our inmates meaningful work, was to have minimum security inmates from Oakhill Correctional Institution take over doing the landscaping and grounds at the state capitol and the governor's mansion. We offered to go further and have them take over the maintenance of state office buildings, but it was rejected because it would displace people with those jobs.

One other set of skills our inmates in various institutions have is the ability to make beautiful furniture and cabinetry. Most people didn't know that it was the inmates that made the reproduction antique furniture located throughout the capitol. They did exemplary work, and when the subject of restoration work in the kitchen at the governor's mansion came up, I offered the services of the inmate craftsmen. Initially, it got some interest but was ultimately dismissed by the First Lady in favor of using money raised by a foundation. I thought that it would have been a great story to tell in years to come that the state had been so frugal in utilizing inmate craftsmen to handle the project. Oh, well, we tried.

When I came into office, I was briefed on a partnership that had been started between the Wisconsin DOC and the country of Armenia, a former Soviet state. That partnership was made at the request of the U.S. State Department's Bureau of International Narcotics and Law Enforcement Affairs (INL). The INL had been working with Armenia on human rights reforms and corrections modernization, which had become critical issues in that country. This was exciting stuff, and I dove right into it. I studied the country, the ethnic issues, and the stories on prison atrocities, as I tried to understand the breadth and depth of the problem. The INL provided me with background on the country and a briefing on the challenges ahead. Ultimately, I would be invited to Armenia to meet with its president and the minister of corrections as they built their first new correctional institution in decades.

While we were working with Armenia, the State Department asked if we would consider also working with the Republic of Georgia, another former Soviet state and neighboring country to Armenia. The mission would be very similar, in that they were desperately in need of human rights and corrections reforms. The entire government of Georgia had essentially collapsed after their own prison atrocities were publicized. I made two trips to Georgia, meeting with their prime minister and becoming friends with the new Minister of Corrections Giorgi Mgebrishvili. Both of those countries were essentially emerging from the dark ages of corrections work, and it was exciting to be there to help them design new facilities, train their staff, draft training protocols, and ultimately have their staff come to Wisconsin to train on our system. It was without a doubt one of the more memorable partnerships I have ever been a part of. However, there was a deeper lesson to be learned from working with those countries. Their entire political landscape changed because of problems in their prison systems. Years of neglect, inaction, and inadequate funding by their government leaders had implications. I could not help but wonder if Scott Walker could learn from that after I explained it to him, which I did. And he did not.

One of the most inspiring aspects of the DOC staff was the

incredible charitable work they did across Wisconsin. In particular, I was very proud of the work they did with Special Olympics Wisconsin. I had been asked to join the board of directors of the Special Olympics and was proud to draw attention to the activities that DOC staff members did across the state in support of their wonderful work. I even offered to do the Special Olympics Polar Plunge with any DOC institution that would put a team together to jump into the frigid winter water. One year, I jumped six times with DOC teams, which my friends thought was crazy. I would intentionally wear a standard DOC officer's uniform to show my solidarity with the frontline staff, and they enjoyed it.

In other fundraising events, I would do whatever I could to participate in the revelry to support charities. My dignity knew no lower limits, and much to the chagrin of some command staff who thought I was denigrating the secretary's office, I gave it my all.

Taking a cabinet appointment with Scott Walker was instructive in who the man was. Unfortunately, it became evident over time that I was the wrong kind of guy to work in his administration. Walker had created a barrier between himself and state employees by pushing through Act 10. It was a barrier he would never try to get past, and in fact, it was a barrier he worked hard to maintain. Looking back at all of Walker's public appearances, his photo opportunities, his visits hither and yon, I cannot recall one where he actually visited a state agency or talked with state employees. That was, I believe, the same persona he wanted his secretaries to maintain. We would be expected to cheer on the conservative firebrand tirelessly, but our concern for the well-being of our staff was to be an afterthought. That was not who I was or ever would be. Walker could go on the campaign trail and denigrate state employees as "the haves" as opposed to "the have-nots," but at the end of the day, his agencies didn't run without them. They deserved respect and consideration, which was not something Walker was willing to give.

Throughout my time with the DOC, I tried to lead with compassion wherever possible. I would attend the funerals of staff and their families when I could, visit people in the hospital, and walk through the institutions at night and on the weekends to talk with staff without their supervisors present. This was something that the wardens were not much in favor of because in some cases they feared what staff would say about them. As I explained to them, if they were out walking around and talking to their staff, then their staff might not feel the need to gripe to me.

I had asked Cheryl early on to reach out to the division administrators and have them notify me when staff members had a loss in their families. With 10,000 employees, I couldn't get to every funeral, but I could at least send them a personal note expressing my condolences and prayers. On one occasion, Cheryl came in to let me know that the baby of one of our officers had passed away after a brief medical episode. The officer was the son of another DOC employee named Mary, and she was the matriarch of a family of DOC staff that made their careers with our agency.

Because I nearly lost my own daughter as a baby, any issue with kids hit me in the gut. I asked Cheryl to find out the funeral arrangements, and I would quietly attend. No entourage, no staff in tow, just me. I didn't want anyone notified that I was attending, because I just wanted to be there as a father, not as a figurehead.

It was a cold and blustery Saturday in Wauzeka, Wisconsin. The temperature was hovering around 20 degrees, and the wind was constant at about 15 miles per hour. I walked into the little church in town that was more the size of a house than the typical church I grew up in. The place was packed, and I quietly fell in line with the others wishing to express their condolences to the grief-stricken parents. I stood out in my suit attire, and a few people started whispering and pointing, most likely DOC staff. When I finally got up to the parents, I shook their hands and expressed my condolences. The father, a DOC officer, looked at me for a minute and asked who I was. I told him I was Ed Wall and worked at DOC headquarters.

His eyes grew wide, and he said, "Secretary Wall?"

I nodded and said, "Today, I'm just Ed Wall." He asked what I was doing there. I just looked at him and his wife and said, "You're facing a tragedy that no parent should have to face. When we stumble, it's important that someone is there to help us up. I just want you to know I'm here." His eyes teared up, and I gave them each a hug and moved to a pew in the middle of the church.

After the Mass, I went to the graveside service. It was bone-chilling cold, and I fortunately had my heavy winter overcoat. As we all shuffled across the frozen ground to the gravesite, the wind swept down the hill, and everyone grabbed their coats, pulling them tighter. I stood back from the crowd a little to let close family and friends be nearest to the grieving parents. Standing in front of me was a thin young man with no coat on. He was shivering, hands jammed into his pockets, and doing his best to stand in respect. I took off my overcoat and put it over his shoulders from behind him. He spun around and started taking the coat off to give back to me saying, "No, sir, I can't take your coat. It's too cold."

I reached over and pulled the coat back over his shivering body and said, "Listen, I have plenty of insulation and a suit coat. I'll just turn my back to the wind like a yak and be just fine. You keep this coat on. Please."

He looked down, giving a forced smile and said, "Thank you." I wouldn't know until weeks later that the young man was the brother of the baby's father and one of our officers in that family of state employees serving the DOC.

That poor family of DOC employees would have tragedy strike them again less than two years later as another one of the brothers, also a DOC officer, lost both daughters in a horrific fire while he and his wife worked third shift; the girls were their only children. in a horrific fire while he and his wife worked third shift. When I received the call at about 3:30 a.m., I got dressed and started heading to the scene in Wauzeka. I shuddered at the thought of what these parents were going through.

When I pulled into town on that freezing winter dawn, the smoldering house on the main street was surrounded by firefighters, first responders, and arson investigators. I went over and spoke to the DCI special agent who was investigating the scene—a man I had known for years. He already knew that the father was one of our officers and just said, "Sorry about your loss, Ed. It looks like it's probably a wood stove issue, but we don't know for sure." I thanked him for his work and headed to Mary's house, where her son and his wife were.

When I walked in, Mary met me at the door, and I just hugged her. She started crying, and I whispered, "I don't know how much one family can endure, but I want you to know that we are here for you; I am here for you." Her son was in a bedroom and came out shortly with his wife, the look of shock evident on their faces. He was a big guy, about my build, but he looked so small as he sat hunched over in the kitchen chair. I hugged his wife, assuring her that we would help them get through this, and she trembled, nodding her thanks, unable to speak.

I walked over to the father and put my arm around his shoulders, and he just sobbed. After a moment he looked up and said, "Secretary, we've lost everything. Our only children are gone. We have nothing. The only thing I have are the clothes I'm wearing," which was his DOC uniform. The prospect of losing everything in life that you treasure is beyond most people's comprehension. Where do you start to help people in that position? I felt helpless despite my attempt to offer comforting words. He looked up at me and said, "I'm going to have to go to the funeral home to make arrangements for my daughters today, and this is all I have," and he started crying again.

I told him I would be right back and went to my state car. There was always an emergency bag of clothes in my trunk. Jeans, a sweater, a T-shirt, underwear, socks, sneakers, and a simple shaving kit with the bare essentials. I also had a brand-new winter coat that I had just bought the day before. Grabbing both, I walked back into the house and said, "This is only a tiny first step, and there will be many more. Here is a change of clothes and a winter coat. It is a start, and you need to know that there is hope." He just nodded appreciation and looked back at the floor, crying. The statewide DOC family would pull together quickly in response. Within hours, clothes were being collected across the state and sent to Wauzeka. The DOC machine was engaged.

I would be flying out of state the next day on business, and Dede would be representing our office at the funeral. When I went home, my wife and kids had already started pulling together extra clothes and filled two large black yard bags with donations that should fit the parents. Additionally, I took out one of my suits, ironed a couple of my dress shirts, picked a few ties, and a pair of dress shoes. Dede would arrive at my house the next morning to pick up the items before I headed out of state. She asked me if I wanted the suit and dress clothes back and I said, "No, he is going to need them, and they are his." As she left, I thought about the prospect of attending your child's funeral in someone else's dress clothes. To this day, it makes me shudder to think about it. ♦

9

CORRECTIONS—
THE SELF-LICKING
ICE CREAM CONE

Corrections is a study in competing challenges. It is the most reviled state agency and yet serves one of the most important missions. Politicians avoid it like the plague, yet they perpetuate the bad press by refusing to invest in better outcomes. The department is either the biggest or one of the biggest users of taxpayer dollars in every state. When the legislature sees the DOC secretary or the budget staff coming toward them, what they see is a cash-eating behemoth looking for more food. In Wisconsin, the DOC biennial budget was about $2.65 billion. People can't fathom the cost of caring for about 22,000 inmates, 90,000 people on probation or parole, and over 10,000 employees. For example, if the Packers made the playoffs or the Super Bowl, the overtime alone would be about a million dollars, as people called in sick. These are the things that other cabinet secretaries and the governor never thought about, until the bills rolled in.

Unfortunately, over the years the DOC had become a self-licking ice cream cone. Whether it is the probation system that perpetuates a continuous cycle of reincarceration on technical violations or staff shortages that create incredible overtime expenses, the entire system feeds on itself. Until a governor and a legislature look at Corrections as something more than a warehouse solution to a crime problem, the self-licking mantra will continue on.

The fact that about 95 percent of all inmates will eventually be returned to society is a sobering fact. Your view of corrections changes once you understand that and connect the dots that prison experience is reflected in recidivism rates. If it doesn't, then you are not paying attention, ignorant, or blinded by a political position that is oblivious to reality.

Most people don't know much about what the DOC does, nor do they really want to know. Depending on your socioeconomic situation, inmates are either your neighbors, relatives, friends, or bad people who live in other areas. Wisconsin has had the unfortunate distinction of incarcerating a disproportionate percentage of African Americans. That is a "number one" ranking that nobody wants to own, but it was ours when I came into office. Of course, the arguments about those statistics will be never-ending. One side claims it was because they committed more crimes, while the other side points to the inequality of opportunities for minorities, the cycle of crime and family issues they deal with, and the perceived biases within the criminal justice system itself.

Coming from an upper-middle-class family with few minorities in my schools and none as my neighbors, I'll admit that my view was not well informed. Even as a cop, I and many of the people I worked with would look down our nose at the people we arrested and chalked it up to another failed minority story. It was not until I went into the DOC that my opinion and education would change dramatically based on the evidence and what I experienced.

I studied the issue and was blessed that my deputy secretary, a black female, was patient with the well-to-do white guy who wanted to effect change. But how do you make those changes when much of the GOP-controlled legislature was uninterested in hearing about minority incarceration rates, and the governor was the lead architect of tough-on-crime legislation? The obvious answer was, "you don't," but that was not acceptable to me.

In my life experience, I knew that faith-based groups could make tremendous impacts on the community, both behind bars and in the neighborhoods where problems brewed. With that, we reached out to religious leaders in Milwaukee and Madison to engage with them and learn what their capabilities were. The DOC had dealt with these faith-based groups for years, but not in the way I wanted to. In my heart, I knew that the engagement must be personal and involve me and my deputy secretary meeting with them face to face to show that the DOC's commitment came from the top down. The deputy secretary and I went on the road often and attended meetings, workshops, job fairs, and counseling sessions with recently released inmates and those at risk of becoming inmates. That is how we were; we needed to be in the trenches where the substantive discussions happened.

The painful reality of incarceration is that unless we as a society embrace making changes in the people we send to prison, they are likely to return to the streets and do precisely what they did before—or worse. There will always be that mentality that prison is supposed to be punishment. Many people would not be happy unless the inmates are breaking rocks or placed in solitary. I get it. Make them pay for their crimes. However, until you come into the corrections orbit, you really don't understand the impact the corrections system has on the "product" that is ultimately released from prison.

If people thought that a prisoner being released was going to live next door to them, would they want a hardened criminal who was treated harshly in a system just for the sake of punishment? Or would they rather have a person who was offered a transformational experience in mental health and addiction programming or job skills training, and who earned a high school diploma to make him more employable? It's easy to want prisoners to be treated harshly to pay for their crimes. That is, until they live next door to you.

Although it would be considered sacrilege to utter these words as a GOP governor's appointee, the work of corrections changes the way even the most conservative minds think if they are fully educated on the issues. It changed me. If you understand the problems and the mechanisms to effectively change them, you will eventually be branded a liberal or a Democrat. I would prefer to be labeled as informed.

In Milwaukee, there is a conservative radio personality with a large following. He sees himself as very important and thinks he is the conscience of the Republican Party. I, however, found him to be an obnoxious, arrogant man who prides himself on bullying people and using his platform to attack others. There was a case of a recently released inmate who was involved in a motorcycle accident. This radio host had been contacted by one or more DOC probation agents who complained that the inmate should have never been released and pointed to the probation rules they didn't like as the cause. He then grabbed that flag and raced up the hill, blaming me for the rules and ranting that every prisoner who commits any violation while on probation should be thrown back in prison.

There was a time when I would have agreed with that radio personality, but that was before I had to run the prison system. It's easy to want everyone locked up. However, it is something else entirely to actually do it in an overcrowded system with no relief valves. He had the luxury of not being encumbered with the realities we had to face in the DOC. He could just scream that everyone should be locked up. He accused me of being a Democrat holdover since I had been appointed by Governor Doyle to run Emergency Management. He repeatedly called for me to be thrown out of my position as not being tough enough on the inmates. He went to great lengths to malign me and questioned the governor's judgment in keeping me in office. He was, in fact, just another uninformed windbag who simply liked to throw grenades and watch the carnage that ensued. He had no real answers, just complaints. In his perfect world, we would just keep building prisons, and the budget would continue to inflate without concern. He didn't have to run anything or account for the results; he just spewed venom.

"Complaining about a problem without proposing a solution is called whining." So said Teddy Roosevelt.

I was receiving calls from many people about what this radio host was saying, and I asked the governor's office to allow me to go on the air with the radio host to try and explain. Every request was denied. Their position was that he is just a jerk, and he will go after the governor. So I was left to sit there and absorb the arrows so that the governor would have coverage. My anger with the situation grew, and finally Eric Schutt asked one of his connections to intercede to stop the attacks. That radio host was, however, like a dog with a bone.

I saw the governor around that time at a social event at the executive residence, and he consoled me on the brutal attacks the radio host was continuing to make because he was also hearing about them. He explained that he couldn't personally stand him either but told me to hang in there and "keep doing what you're doing." He then used his own situation and the Act 10 protests to illustrate how we needed to have tough skin when it came to the media. Having thick skin was not the problem; the problem was that I could not defend my agency with facts and the law against an onslaught by a media guy who claimed to be an ally of the governor. By having me absorb the hits, the governor maintained his deniability, a talent he had refined. Where I came from, that was called cowardice. You either own it or you don't. If he wanted changes made, he could have directed me to make those changes at any time, and they would have been made. Instead, the governor and his staff did what they often did and hoped it would all just pass by, leaving the ravaged secretary bleeding at the curb as their bus pulled away.

The governor's office also made life more difficult in dealing with the corrections unions, which were still stinging from Act 10. When I first came into office, I was contacted by Executive Director Marty Beil of the AFSCME union. Marty and I had known each other since I was in the union years earlier. He asked if I would be available to meet him for breakfast to discuss some outstanding issues he had. I agreed, and we set a date to get together a few days later.

I called the governor's office to let them know that I was going to be meeting with Beil and got a call back a short time later from Director of Communications Jocelyn Webster, telling me that I was not to meet with Beil under any circumstances and chastised me for thinking it was a good idea. Easy for her to say, not having to run our agency. Subsequently, I sent Marty an email advising that I would have to cancel the breakfast. As I expected, he was angry, and this got us off on the wrong foot and led to an ongoing antagonistic relationship between my office and the union that did not need to happen. But it was all about appearances and not substance; that was the mantra of the governor's office.

Throughout my time as secretary of the DOC, we prepared and presented multiple plans for modernization and cost savings to the governor's office. The largest issue for the DOC was a combination of aging institutions and exploding populations. We drew up a master plan for the governor's review that involved building a single, large campus of institutions ranging from minimum to maximum security. That campus would have a centralized medical facility, transportation infrastructure, and educational and mental health facilities. This would allow the DOC to sell off multiple facilities across the state where inefficiencies were pervasive.

Older institutions were made with poor sight lines, alcoves, alleys, and areas where danger could lurk. Their mechanical systems were often outdated and expensive to maintain. New facility designs benefited from improvements in construction, technology, and safety. Additionally, they were much less expensive to operate as far fewer staff were needed because of the improvements in managed custody. We had proposed building a campus like that with a projected savings of over $500 million over 15 years, but it was rejected by the governor's chief of staff, Rich Zipperer. Why? "Nobody wanted to be seen as the politician who put more money into Corrections." Corrections issues didn't garner votes, so it was easier just to keep backing up trucks full of cash and dumping them on the front lawn under the auspices of "cost to continue." I often wondered if Zipperer kept those plans we left with him on the issues DOC proposed. It would be interesting to find out, but I am guessing that they quickly found their way to a shredder. Because as I would learn: No records, no problems. ♟

LIFE IN THE CABINET AND THE GAME OF THRONES

B eing a cabinet secretary should be considered an honor. In the perfect world, you would think that the best people available would be chosen to lead the state agencies that work to serve the citizen taxpayers. When I was offered the daunting role as DOC secretary, I was shocked but also humbled that the governor thought enough of my leadership abilities to ask me to lead his largest and arguably most volatile cabinet agency.

What I would unfortunately learn was that being picked for the DOC secretary position was more like being identified as a sacrificial lamb that would be disposed of when the going got rough. Or, should I say, when the press started mentioning an agency's problems and Walker's name in the same sentence. Where I came from, when under fire, you worked with your partner to resolve the crisis. Where Walker came from, when you were under fire, you pushed your partner out in front of the bullets hoping the shooter would get tired of shooting him instead of you.

Unfortunately, within a year it became obvious that although I was told I would have the ability to run the DOC, the truth was much different. We were increasingly micromanaged by the governor's office, which was staffed with a lot of inexperienced youngsters or others hoping for positions of power. They were good at gazing with adoration at their governor, but they had no idea what they were doing with regard to Corrections. For those interested in ever becoming the DOC secretary under an administration like Walker's, take a tip from me: Your opinion and sense of what is right and wrong don't matter. If your experience and knowledge lead you to a different understanding of the agency after you have entered office, either hold it inside or resign. Because your position is nothing more than being a cheerleader for political catchphrases and pledges your boss made while pandering for votes. You will have to accept that there will be no interest in addressing Corrections problems you raise unless:

a. The state gets sued with the governor and legislature obligated to react.

b. There is an impending election, and those problems are in the news.

c. There is a real possibility that their inaction will demonstrate incompetence.

d. In any case above, understand it will be your fault.

At my first cabinet meeting, there were chairs arranged all around the perimeter of the room where the secretary's support staff and deputy secretaries sat. It was all quite formal. It was amusing to watch people jockeying for seats on the perimeter, all in hopes of being seen by the governor or chief of staff.

When the governor came in, everyone took their seats, and the adoring eyes all turned toward him. The governor opened by introducing me as the new DOC secretary, and I stood up and turned around to see everyone in the room. I was met with a round of applause. The governor had some very nice remarks about my exemplary career in law enforcement and how lucky they were that I accepted the appointment. "How did I ever end up here?" was all I could think of. I wondered what my parents would have thought at that moment if they had lived long enough to see it. Would my dad have been impressed by what his son, who only wanted to be a cop, had become? My eyes watered up as I took my seat, thinking of them and not the well-wishers' clapping hands.

The cabinet meetings always started with the governor opening the meeting, if he was there. Often, he was not at the meetings. If he was not there, the chief of staff would run the meeting in a pretty business-like manner.

When the governor was there, the atmosphere was different. The secretaries would be a bit more enthusiastic and ingratiating in their agency briefings, usually giving credit to the governor for any good news they had to deliver. In some cases, it was embarrassing to watch these fawning performances. That was not the case with the DOC. Our news was typically a bit more realistic and never filled with rainbows or unicorns. My intention was never to impress or leave a vision that everything was just wonderful, because it was not. We had serious responsibilities and serious issues to deal with. The other secretaries would pay attention when I gave our briefings, their eyes wide as I spoke about the challenges we faced. As time would go on, my hesitation to share the real needs of the department would decrease. There could be no doubt in anyone's mind about the dire need our department was facing, and that would eventually be my undoing because I wouldn't paint a smiley face on our agency. We required the governor and legislature's help, and I made that clear.

You never knew who all the people in the room were, and sometimes that would inspire guarded conversation by the secretaries. However, when we had the secretary-only meetings or dinners at the governor's mansion, it was a different story. The conversations were often colorful and could be very frank with regard to expectations from the administration. When the governor wasn't present, those conversations could be even more animated. The facade of effusive praise for the governor and the administration's actions that were usually on display in the general cabinet meetings could give way to honest opinion and concerns. That was a quality that would erode over time, but personally, I was never one to mince words or sugarcoat my observations.

It was always clearly stated that our job was to make the governor look good. We should try and secure media attention when possible that pointed to his accomplishments. We should coordinate op-ed articles with the governor's office and look for public speaking engagements that offered the opportunity to praise the "big, bold reforms" that had been made.

Cabinet meetings were an interesting study of personalities and power. It was indeed a *Game of Thrones*, as secretaries jockeyed for positions closest to the governor's. Unlike me, most of the secretaries were former Republican politicians. Some had no experience in the areas they were appointed to, but that wouldn't matter if they were loyal and willing to effusively praise the boss and fall on their sword if needed. It was clear that the bigger concern was for party loyalty and an understanding of how to navigate the minefield of Republican legislators who could derail the administration's goals and objectives.

There wasn't too much concern for Democratic opinions because they seemed to be insignificant considering the majority the Republicans held. That feeling was even more empowered after the gerrymandering exercise of redistricting that the legislature had gone through. I would hear other secretaries who had been politicians talking about their former districts, very content with how the party had cemented their seats for the GOP. It was not about fair representation; it was about the party and manipulating the votes tallies. As a citizen interested in the fair election of representatives, I remember looking at the redistricting issues and thinking, "I can't believe what lengths these people will go to assure their own survival." In my mind, I thought it would be far fairer just to lay a grid on the state and divide things up that way. That's probably why I would make a terrible politician and never cared very much for them. My whole life had been about doing what was right, not what was expedient or taken from a political handbook on power control.

At my core, I believed in communication. Throughout my career, as a cop and with the Division of Criminal Investigation and at Emergency Management, I didn't mince words or sit on my haunches waiting for others to make decisions; I communicated, made a decision, and moved. It was part of being an effective problem-solver. You can't be a leader if you're always waiting for someone else to make a move. Just like police work, things can change in an instant when working in corrections. A calm day can turn into a crisis in the blink of an eye. On average, we had 10 officers a week assaulted across the state. Those assaults could range from urine and feces being thrown on an officer to stabbings or worse. These situations all had to be dealt with, and communicating was crucial.

In November 2013, one of our best DOC attorneys announced she was leaving, and we had an attorney position that would be posted to fill. It was not long after that when I received a call from Attorney General J.B. Van Hollen. He wasted no time in telling me that he was calling to let me know that his wife, Lynne, was interested in the open attorney position at the DOC. He opined that they hoped to have a steady income with insurance while he started his own consulting work after the upcoming election, because he had announced he was not running for re-election. I told him that I was not typically involved in hiring decisions and encouraged him to have her apply and go through the process. He took a moment to remind me that he had hired me into my dream job as DCI administrator and inferred that I basically owed him as a result. It was a very uncomfortable feeling, knowing that the attorney general, the state's "Top Cop," was putting the arm on me to hire his wife to repay him for a civil service, competitive appointment as DCI administrator. I again encouraged him to have her apply, knowing that we typically got very few lawyers applying to the DOC because of the low pay.

The exchange with J.B. was so uncomfortable that I asked my deputy secretary to keep me isolated from the process entirely and leave the decision up to the legal chief on hiring. Subsequently, Lynne applied, and my legal chief advised that she had come up as the top candidate. Lynne had good experience and interviewed well, so the decision was an honest one based on merit, and more importantly, one that I did not make. She came on board in January 2014 and overall did a good job for us. After about two weeks on the job, Lynne came to me and took the time to share what her perceptions were of the office environment, the legal chief, the pros and cons of her peers, and what she thought needed to be done to fix it. All in two weeks! Wow.

As time would go on, some more ripples appeared on the pond, and I started hearing from other attorneys that Lynne was sometimes difficult to work with. I also heard from outside sources that she had aggravated some agencies with her attitude and demeanor. This didn't bother me too much, because I knew from experience that lawyers could be aggravating. What did start to bother me was Lynne's continued advocacy to be allowed to work from home a few days a week. This was just something I could not support, considering how overworked our attorneys were and the fact that people like to speak with their legal staff face to face when possible.

Several months later, my legal chief announced her retirement, and I was very sorry to see her go. She had been a well-respected, considerate, and very experienced attorney for the DOC, and she would be missed greatly. She had ascended to the legal chief position after Kevin Potter, the former legal chief, was appointed by none other than J.B. Van Hollen as administrator of Legal Services at the DOJ. That was an unclassified political appointment by an elected official, and therefore, Kevin had restoration rights back to the legal chief position in the DOC that were protected by state law and DOA policy MRS-211. These were the same laws and policies that protected my own restoration after my cabinet appointment was completed, and I considered them irrevocable.

Once Lynne heard that my legal chief was retiring, I received a call not long after from J.B. advocating that I put his wife into the legal chief position. I explained to J.B. that Kevin Potter, his own appointee, had restoration rights back to that position, and I would hold it open until Kevin advised me of his intentions, likely after the election. J.B. didn't like that answer, probably because he would no longer be in office to exert pressure when the decision was made.

He then said, "You can put Potter in another position instead, just like I could move you out of the DCI administrator position if I wanted to if you came back." That was a horrible harbinger of things to come. I disagreed with J.B. on his interpretation of the law and told him so. It was the same twisting of the law that he tried to do with Jim Warren. We parted ways on that disagreement, and I have never spoken to him since. Alas, once the politician was done with you, you are discarded like yesterday's trash.

This ideology that J.B. expressed was contrary to the well-established laws and state policies of restoration. However, I was not surprised that this was his take on those laws since he wanted his wife to get a nice pay raise. Politicians often express surprise when they are told there are laws against things they may be trying to do. Sometimes they are even inclined to change those laws once they find out it applies to them. And if you were a politician who was also the attorney general, then those laws are subject to your own interpretation, since you had a building full of lawyers to argue on your behalf, right or wrong.

J.B., however, took it one step further. He tried to go around me to the governor's chief of staff, Eric Schutt. J.B. told Eric that I had "promised" the legal chief job to his wife, which was an absolute fabrication. Not only had I not promised her any job, but I had taken the time to explain why I would wait to fill it until I heard from the man that had restoration rights to the position after J.B. was gone. Eric called me and related the call from J.B., and I explained the reality of our conversations. Eric was not surprised and left the decision up to me as it was a direct appointment I would make as secretary.

Ultimately, Kevin decided to stay at the DOJ in a civil service deputy administrator position to finish out his years of state service. I ended up appointing Julio Barron, who was a retired colonel in the U.S. Air Force, had been the staff judge advocate for the Wisconsin Department of Military Affairs, and a former assistant attorney general in Minnesota. His experience, candor, personality, and drive were what we needed at the DOC, and we were fortunate to be able to get him to come on board. Lynne was not very happy, and her chagrin was noticeable. She approached the new legal chief more than once and continued to ask to be allowed to work from home a few days a week. After she was denied every time, she eventually resigned and left the DOC. I knew that I had created an enemy with a powerful GOP politician because I did what was right and not politically correct. It would be part of a tremendous bill to pay down the road.

Before the governor entered his second term, despite what he had been saying to the press, every person in the cabinet knew that Walker would be running for president. In the late spring of 2014, over a year before he would announce his intention to run for president, Walker decided to write a book. That book, titled *Unintimidated: A Governor's Story and a Nation's Challenge*, was obviously being crafted as a thinly disguised springboard for his entry onto the national stage. Walker, or rather his GOP fundraising machine, had a story to tell that focused on the upheaval of Act 10 and the "right to work" movement. The book was actually written by Marc Thiessen, who had been brought in to play up the wonderful story of "big, bold reforms" that Walker had steamrolled through the legislature.

Chief of Staff Eric Schutt called me one day and asked if I would be able to come in on that Saturday to sit with him, the governor, Mike Huebsch, Keith Gilkes, and Marc Thiessen to recount the experiences of the Act 10 actions and responses. We all spent that Saturday in the governor's office going over the issues that we each faced throughout the Act 10 protests. In the book that followed, my recollections were noted, and I was mentioned a few times for my part in handling the law enforcement response. When I came home that day, my wife asked how it went. I shared with her my thoughts that the book was typical of politicians who saw their own stars rising and wanted to showcase their credentials for the world to see. I also thought the book would highlight that Walker was, in reality, a one-trick pony for the big national conservative funders he was performing for.

Subsequently, when the book was published, I was told by Eric Schutt that I could get a copy of the book if I wanted one, but I would have to pay for it! The small number of free books Walker would receive would be given to large money donors. I donated most of a Saturday, away from my family, to help Walker on his "look at me" self-aggrandizement marketing effort, and he wanted me to buy the book? I told Eric, "Thanks anyway," and that I had better things to do with my money. Unbeknownst to me, my wife bought a copy of the book and arranged to get it signed by the governor. When I found out that Walker was charging for signing the books and charged even more for personal notes, I was very disappointed, but she was able to get the note and signature for free. It said, "Ed, thank you for your leadership at DOC—and for your help at DOJ in the past!"

Several months before the November 2014 election, I was in Eric's office discussing a few issues. I asked him outright, "Do you think he's going to run for president?" I asked because the governor kept telling people he intended to serve his term if he was re-elected.

Eric looked at me and said, "That decision was made a long time ago. He's running." I wasn't surprised but often wondered how many people would have voted for him in the second election if they knew he was just using his position as governor as a stepping-stone out of the state. Unfortunately, later when I thought about *Unintimidated*, it left me *uninspired*, which was to be the original title of this book. I never found the time to read Walker's book.

What the governor was doing reminded me of J.B. Van Hollen "dialing for dollars" and asking for donations to his campaign, knowing he wasn't going to seek re-election. I was with J.B. when we were traveling together to some event, and he had me stop so he could get out of the state car to make those calls. I asked him how he could ask people for money to support his campaign, since he had shared with me he probably wouldn't seek re-election well over a year before. He simply said that his campaign owed him money that he had lent to it during his first run for office. He wanted to get repaid, and he saw it as a debt that his supporters owed him. I remember thinking, "They owed you?" How about the fact you wanted the position and power enough to pay for it? With Walker and Van

Hollen, their actions were nothing short of disingenuous and self-serving. The only interest was what was in it for themselves, not what was truthful or the right thing to do.

Politicians of all shapes and sizes are perennially focused on the next election or the next high office they will go after. It was always about power, which they referred to as their "desire to govern." The problem with career politicians is that they become talking heads who respond to polls and pressure from big money donors.

On many occasions, I would be called to state senators' offices from both sides of the aisle. They would sometimes berate me about the size of our budget, or they would inquire about programs, complaints, or incarcerated constituents, or they would attempt to get me to deliver a message to the governor because they could not get through to him. You see, they had to get re-elected also and if they couldn't pull the strings of the other puppets in the show, then their own future was in jeopardy.

It's the gang mentality of political parties that gives them strength, and in this way, they are like labor unions. Republican officials hated the unions because they were groups of people who banded together to watch out for their own future and survival, which was no different than what they did. In effect, political parties are the ultimate unions, and their knives come out quickly for any one of their members who doesn't toe the line. That's why successful "independent" politicians are as rare as hairy frogs.

During my visits with those legislators I took lots of notes, promised to do my best, and relayed messages to the governor's office as requested. Sometimes these meetings were productive, but often I just served as a punching bag for the frustration that legislators of both parties had with my boss. The concern was growing within the governor's office that even the Republicans' support for him seemed to be tenuous at times, which only got worse after he announced his presidential run. As that chasm began to widen, the governor's office ratcheted up its micromanagement of cabinet agencies—in particular, those that attracted negative media, like the DOC. ❧

LINCOLN HILLS

It was a dark day in the DOC's history when I was notified by my staff about the allegations of abuse of youth inmates brought to us by the Milwaukee County district attorney's office. I was advised that we did not have the names of any victims or suspected staff. The length of time this had been going on was also unknown.

Putting on my former DCI administrator hat, I told them that we needed to try and identify any potential victims and the officers involved as soon as possible. Once we had that information, we would then set the investigation in motion. I asked the Office of Special Operations (OSO) to take control of the investigation so that people at the institution would not be investigating it themselves. We could not afford to have the appearance of impropriety attached to this because the implications were too big.

Shortly thereafter, I got in my car and traveled to the capitol to meet with Eric Schutt to alert him about what we had been advised of. Sensitive to the moratorium on creating records, I didn't dare put it into an email considering the potential negative press it could stir up. I told Eric that my inclination was to ask the DCI to investigate this if there was merit to the accusations, and he agreed. Likewise, I notified DOA Secretary Mike Huebsch and advised him of my intentions, which he also concurred with. Eric and Mike both understood the importance of this potential case and deferred to my law enforcement experience in how to run the investigation.

It took several weeks for the DOC to conduct interviews and gather information with potential victims, some of whom were initially reluctant to come forward. Eventually, a few potential victims were identified, and the names of some officers allegedly involved were also determined. When Dede and the juvenile corrections administrator came back to brief me on January 14, 2015, they shared the information the OSO had gathered, indicating some troubling descriptions of officers running "fight clubs" amongst the youth offenders and rewarding them with candy bars and such. My stomach turned at the thought, and we immediately grasped the severity of the situation. I moved forward with the request that the DCI investigate the case. It was the only agency with statewide criminal investigative authority, and victims could be anywhere.

I immediately called Dave Matthews, who was the DCI administrator while I was in my gubernatorial appointment. I explained what we were working on and asked him if the DCI would be willing to take the case. Dave was very reluctant and said he thought this was more of an "internal affairs issue," which I disagreed with. I explained to Dave that this case could have enormous consequences for the state and our agency if state employees were harming youth in our custody. Besides, I explained that interviews would have to be conducted in a variety of locations, and criminal actions could be very likely. Dave was still reluctant, and I sensed his apprehension over getting involved with the DOC, but he subsequently relented and agreed to look into it. We planned to have the DCI staff meet with our OSO staff to go over the case. What should have been a harbinger of things to come, the DOJ would schedule its first meeting with DOC staff nine days later on January 23, 2015. So much for prompt attention to a critical situation.

From the very beginning, the DOC made it clear to the DOJ that we wanted this investigation to be expedited because of the explosive allegations that state employees could be harming youth in our care. However, the DOJ continued to give us lip service for months and was less than transparent in how they were handling the case. About two weeks into the "investigation," they warned us that this would not be a fast case. In fact, on more than one occasion, they called us to advise that the Lincoln Hills investigation would be "on the back burner" for a while as other high-profile cases arose. I was fuming and could not understand who was making the call at the DOJ that youth potentially being harmed by state employees should take a "back burner" to anything else.

At the same time the investigation was kicking off, the new attorney general, Brad Schimel, was just coming into office. I had not known Schimel before he ran for office. When I first met with him, he came across as a good guy. He had announced publicly that he had appointed his friend, Brian O'Keefe, who I had arranged to get the political appointment as DOJ administrator of Law Enforcement Services, as his transition director for his incoming administration. Brad was excited about being attorney general and asked me some personal questions about Dave Matthews, who had taken my position while I was on gubernatorial appointment. My observations were candid, but I would have never guessed then what Schimel had in mind down the road.

Additionally, I gave Schimel a personal brief on the issues surrounding Lincoln Hills, which I had recently asked the DCI to investigate. I explained that Matthews seemed to act like the case was an imposition, and I wanted to make sure we made it clear to him that this was a priority for our department, and we would do whatever we could to assist. He didn't seem like he had heard much about the investigation before, but it was early in his term, and I didn't know how deeply he drilled into these types of issues. But there is no doubt that when he left my office, he knew exactly how important that investigation was to our agency. It would be later that I would realize elected officials didn't really want to know facts because they lost deniability in knowing. They preferred to be aloof and pleasantly disengaged, which Schimel and Walker would demonstrate over and over in the months and years to come.

The person who appeared to be Schimel's primary handler was Paul Connell, a former assistant U.S. attorney. Schimel brought Connell in and gave him a new position and the title "senior counsel," which had never existed before. He was essentially the third in charge of the DOJ. Over time, I would make a personal conclusion that Connell shared primary responsibility for many of the failings the DOJ would make in the Lincoln Hills investigation.

As a general rule, the secretary's office would not be involved with internal investigations, placing people on leave, disciplinary actions, or terminations. The agency was just too big. On average, the DOC terminated about 20 people per month for cause, almost none of which had anything to do with the secretary's office. Dede offered to oversee the Lincoln Hills case so that it wouldn't look like I was wading in with my home agency, the DCI, in conducting the investigation. It was imperative to me and the DOC that this investigation be completely above board, transparent, and rapidly attended to. Unfortunately, that was not the position of Schimel and the DOJ.

A few weeks after the DOJ started the investigation, Dede came to me and expressed her concern that the DOJ was not taking the case seriously. She said they seemed only to be working part-time on it and feared that we would be crucified if one of the youth were harmed while they dragged their feet with a part-time effort on such an important issue. I asked that she speak directly with the DOJ and DCI management staff to express those concerns. I also asked that we make sure that we were noting the progress of DCI and our actions as an agency. Out of frustration, Dede subsequently set up biweekly conference calls with the DOJ, which would include their investigator, the supervisor, and the assistant attorney general they were working with. Unfortunately, those meetings would be of little help to our agency or the kids at Lincoln Hills.

Early on, I began expressing my frustrations with the governor's office about the lack of progress and information sharing that the DOJ was engaging in on Lincoln Hills. It seemed like the only people who were concerned about the case and the outcomes were at the DOC. We explained to the governor's staff time and again that the implications of the allegations could have widespread negative impacts on the agency and the governor. If it were not that important to us, I would not have immediately driven to the governor's office to tell them in person what was going on and bring in an independent agency to investigate. Yet, we were left feeling completely defenseless. The governor's office just stood back and did not want to get involved, and I feared that by the time they did decide to get involved, the barn would be ablaze.

As the co-chair with the attorney general on the governor's Criminal Justice Coordinating Council, I would speak with Schimel every time we met, before, during, and after the meetings. Each time, I would ask him to please check on the status of the Lincoln Hills investigation, and I pointed out how sensitive this case was to our agency and the governor. He never got back to me once after I would mention it to him. It was becoming painfully obvious that he shared the opinion that it was not important.

Never one to lean toward conspiracy theories, I unfortunately felt myself wondering why it appeared that neither the governor's office nor the DOJ seemed to care about Lincoln Hills. In the back of my mind, I wondered if perhaps that was by design, and the lack of effort was an agreed-upon arrangement behind a closed door to keep the heat off the politicians who were responsible for investigating and fixing the problems. Were they just hoping it would go away? That the press would move on?

As the case crawled along, we began hearing from the staff and supervisors at Lincoln Hills that the atmosphere at the institution was growing increasingly raucous. The youth were all talking amongst themselves about a DOJ investigator who was asking questions about officers harming kids at the institution. This continued to escalate, and many of the youth started claiming they were also being beaten and harmed. It certainly seemed like the DOJ part-time effort was taking its toll on the climate inside the facility. When youth start acting out, it leads to staff tightening down controls, and the friction causes problems for everyone involved. But that wasn't the DOJ's problem; it was ours.

The DOC was very good at keeping records. The Lincoln Hills investigation was no different. From the beginning of February into May 2015, the DOJ would keep telling the DOC that their investigation "continued," though they would offer little meaningful information. At every conference call with the DOJ, our staff would ask, "Is there anyone else we need to put out on leave?" and they would say "no" or offer no information. It was maddening. Was the answer "no" because they did not find any other people who may be under suspicion? Or was the answer "no" because the DOJ had done no further work on the case since they last spoke with the DOC?

On May 12, 2015, the DOJ advised the DOC that their casework was coming to an end soon. Then on May 26, 2015, they advised that 95 percent of the case was completed, but they had concerns that the DOC should not jeopardize the DOJ's case. That was an interesting concern since we didn't know what their case was. I spoke with Dave Matthews at that time, and he advised me that the DOJ was opening a John Doe investigation on the Lincoln Hills case, which we welcomed with open arms. We were praying that perhaps they would get this investigation moving in a manner consistent with the exposure the agency and the state were subjected to.

On June 12, 2015, the DOJ advised the DOC that their case was "transitioning to the prosecution phase," and the DOC could begin its own internal investigation, as we had wanted to for months. The fact that they stated they were moving to the prosecution phase further reinforced what Matthews had told me about the DOJ opening a John Doe investigation. At that time, the DOJ provided the DOC with a list of people whom we could not have contact with, which we assumed was because they were subject to the John Doe secrecy rules.

Another bad assumption.

On June 30, 2015, the DOJ advised that they had a few remaining staff interviews to conduct, but they were moving toward a conclusion. A month later, on July 29, 2015, the DOJ advised the DOC that their investigation was complete, and the attorneys were conferring on the next steps. Finally! However, they would not tell us what they found. I contacted Chief of Staff Eric Schutt and Deputy Chief of Staff Rich Zipperer to advise them both that we finally might have some action taken by the DOJ. Both Eric and Rich were very aware of my angst with the DOJ's plodding nature in the investigation. But nothing happened. The DOJ went dark once again and left us wondering what was happening.

Meanwhile, at a cabinet meeting shortly before the governor announced his presidential run, which we all already knew, Eric told us with somewhat of a resigned tone in his voice, "Listen folks, for the foreseeable future, you just need to run your agencies. Keep your heads low, stay out of the press, and just focus on the business. Don't comment to the press on the governor's presidential campaign and just push ahead."

I recall sitting there listening to the caution about staying out of the press and thinking, "That's not going to happen," because their refusal to engage on Lincoln Hills was going to turn the whole affair into a media circus.

On July 13, 2015, Walker announced that he was, in fact, running for president, which was the worst-kept secret in the country by that time. Democrats immediately went on the attack, and the state Republicans grew somewhat pensive after the official announcement. I know from speaking with some of those legislators that they felt the governor was abandoning them and their Republican majority for his own enrichment at their expense. As his short-lived presidential campaign continued, those feelings of anger would grow exponentially—just as the press coverage of Lincoln Hills started to catch fire.

In early August, after we had been told by the DOJ that their investigation had wrapped up, I received a call from Lincoln County

Sheriff Jeff Jaeger. Jeff told me that his detective sergeant had spoken to some of the Lincoln Hills staff, who advised him the atmosphere at the institution was getting further out of control. I told Jeff that he and I should visit the institution ourselves and make an assessment. My assistant cleared my schedule, and the next day we made our visit, unannounced.

We toured through the institution, and as we walked across the grounds, a few of the youth were yelling to me as they were being moved from their housing units to school. One said, "Hey, we are being tortured!" Another said he was getting beaten up. I stopped and turned to the DOC staff with us, and they said this had become the norm when they saw anyone who appeared to be from the outside.

We walked into the library, and there was a group of youth reading and using the library iPads for studying. As I came in, I said, "Hey fellas, how is it going?" and immediately a group formed around me. Most of the kids knew who I was because I had been up there several times, toured the cottages, and sat in on classes with some of them.

Once I had spoken, they spontaneously started saying that people were being beaten, tortured, and pepper-sprayed throughout the institution, describing broken arms and other injuries. I held up my hand to stop the barrage of accusations and asked each one of them individually if they had personally been assaulted or harmed in any way, and all said they had not. I asked them who had been assaulted or hurt, and they could offer no information beyond, "I heard about this guy ..." and "Someone in another cottage."

I listened patiently to each one of the youth. After spending time and engaging in conversations with the kids, I encouraged them all to write to Deputy Secretary Morgan or me and share any information they had so we could make sure that it was followed up on. I asked the librarian to please send any information the kids wanted to share directly to me, and he acknowledged that request. None was ever received.

What I was seeing was exactly what I feared would be the effects of the DOJ's casual, lingering investigation. The youth were getting riled up, and it was getting difficult to discern what was actually going on. Once again, my frustration grew with the trouble the DOJ had exacerbated but didn't have to deal with.

On August 4, 2015, the DOJ advised the DOC that this would be their last briefing to our agency, and they could not tell us anything. Eight months of investigation and they couldn't tell us anything? They also advised that the staff list they gave the DOC not to contact had been lifted, and we could continue our internal investigation while having no idea what they had found or who they would be prosecuting.

Throughout my time as the DOC secretary, I had asked the governor's office multiple times if Walker could visit some of our institutions or field offices as a sign of support for the agency. Every single time, the idea was dismissed immediately. While Lincoln Hills was dragging along, I asked several times that he consider making an appearance at the institution to demonstrate his commitment to fixing the problems, but again I was told there was no way he would go near the place. All I kept hearing was Jocelyn Webster saying, "Nothing good comes out of Corrections," and I was never sure if that was her position or the governor's, but Walker certainly seemed to be living by it.

In contrast to most governors, Walker kept himself isolated from his cabinet in some regards, which I think was a huge mistake. In speaking with past secretaries in other governors' cabinets, they all said they had regular contact with their governors to work on state business. Cabinet secretaries are responsible for overseeing the most important functions of government, and you would think that governors should be in frequent contact with them. Walker's gaze, however, was fixed on a bigger brass ring than what could be found on the small merry-go-round of Wisconsin. He had fallen prey to the infatuation he and his cash-bundling handlers created with conservatives over Act 10. He was being moved with the strings pulled by the huge money donors who saw this folksy Midwestern guy with the polished delivery as a handy vehicle for getting their policies enacted nationwide. Walker was just a delivery device for somebody else's message, but he obviously thought they loved *him*.

I remember when Walker was suckered into the phony phone call with a radio personality he thought was one of the Koch brothers during the protests around Act 10. I just laughed to myself and thought how shameful it was that politicians were so willing to prostitute themselves to the donors they hoped would help them in the future. It crossed my mind then that Act 10 was probably spoon-fed to Walker by those donors and was nothing more than an effort to catapult himself onto the national stage. And I believe today that is exactly what it was all about.

After Walker was elected for his second term and the wheels were turning toward his presidential ambitions, it became more apparent that just about every action he was taking at the state level was designed to fuel his presidential bid. Draconian budget cuts, lowered taxes, reduction in services, education cuts—all were part of his "Big, Bold Initiatives" campaign slogan. Although that sounded great in his ads, it made running state agencies very difficult.

Time and time again, in cabinet meetings we would discuss the impacts of the continued cuts we were expected to absorb. When the Legislative Fiscal Bureau forecasts were coming out, it was always a rush to use magical math to try and explain things in a different light. Every cabinet agency was pushed to cut more at every turn, but no reasonable ideas were put forth to deal with raising funding. Department of Transportation Secretary Mark Gottlieb expressed his concerns as often as I did, and neither of us received much support. When we were discussing the issues surrounding transportation funding, I asked, "Why don't we look at tolls, just at the interstate entries into the state?" You could have heard a pin drop as all heads turned toward the governor, who just looked at me. I explained my rationale that I couldn't drive through Illinois without hitting a toll every few feet, yet in Wisconsin we were wide open and starving for highway funding. I would be told later that this would be seen as a tax, and there was no way Walker would agree to it. It wasn't about fixing the problem; it was about appearances and political tag lines.

Governor Walker was unfortunately too addicted to his tax-cutting political mantra to accept that he was starving state agencies and critical projects. He would lob the grenade of tax cuts and reduced state budgets, then stand back and watch the legislature take the heat as they tried to fix his mess. Mark Gottlieb and I would eventually pay the price for having the audacity of trying to speak truth to power.

When the news broke about the University of Wisconsin's "hidden cash" accounts, Walker attended the cabinet meeting. He came into the room looking rather chipper, smiles decorating the faces of the cabinet secretaries and their staff, knowing that something big was coming. I could never figure out what Walker's issue was with the UW system, but he always seemed angry with it. Maybe it was because he never finished college himself, or maybe because of the liberal label the UW had arguably earned. In any case, he came to the cabinet meeting advising that he intended to make the UW pay for their deceptive behavior in hiding their money while telling the state they needed more. It was time for retribution. Ultimately, he would freeze tuition, reduce their budget, and make them jump through various hoops to get their funding.

Now, as a parent with college-aged kids, I did not think that was a bad idea. Having been a UW college student and a state employee, I knew the deals that many professors had were beyond reasonable to the common taxpayer. In one of my classes, the professor showed up for the first class and maybe twice more for brief periods throughout the semester, while his teaching assistants taught most of the classes. When the newspaper started publishing state employee pay, I was shocked to read what that professor was making, considering how little I thought he worked. The governor recognized that raw taxpayer nerve and seized upon it; he was good at that kind of thing.

While he was running for president, many of us in the cabinet were frustrated with the inability to make progress on important issues. In my meetings with Chief of Staff Eric Schutt, I could sense his frustration too. Eric shared with me that he did not think Walker had a prayer of winning the election, but he was worried about the negative impact it would have on the governor and the legislature. The issues Wisconsin was dealing with would be of little interest to the presidential candidate as people swooned over him and his newfound fame and various starry-eyed staff went running for the opportunity to be on the "big" campaign.

At one cabinet meeting during his short-lived presidential bid, Walker stopped in to make an appearance. Cabinet secretaries who were previously politicians felt honored that he would take time out of his campaign to grace us with his presence, and they fawned over him. Before the meeting started, I happened to be close to the governor. I said, "Looks like you are getting some pretty positive press, Governor."

"Yeah, but I think I'm peaking too soon," he said. I wished him luck, took my seat, and watched the political groupies in the room gaze in a trance-like state at the man who would be king. He didn't stay in the meeting long, though. He had to leave for an interview with Fox News.

Personally, I never thought he had a chance at becoming president. He did not finish his college degree, he was a professional politician, never having held a job in the "real world," and the sense I had was the public was tired of politicians. He did not have the broad experience or depth of understanding that you would expect in a president. Simply being a folksy Midwestern governor did not equate to presidential readiness in my book, or many others apparently.

In September 2015, as Walker's presidential campaign was crumbling, there was a seminal change in the governor's office with the departure of Chief of Staff Eric Schutt. Eric was superb in his role and mastered the ability to juggle multiple running chainsaws at one time. However, his level of performance was taking a visible toll on him, and his family was undoubtedly paying the price for his incredible work ethic. I was genuinely sorry to see him leave and wondered what our relationship would be with the governor's office after he left. Unfortunately, it would not be good, and many of us felt that the Lincoln Hills debacle would have been handled much better with Eric at the helm in the governor's office.

Truth be told, after Eric left and Rich Zipperer came in as chief of staff, I had to admit to myself that I might not be able to stay in the administration. My frustration had been building for months, and the governor who had asked me to answer his call to leadership was not what he had appeared to be. He had taken me in hook, line, and sinker, based on our one-on-one interactions and his message consistency. It became too apparent that his actions and words were all carefully crafted to keep him protected. In my mind, it was a struggle of conscience. Could I work for a man who I was becoming convinced was an unethical political manipulator?

When Eric was the chief of staff, the cabinet members felt they had an outlet to speak honestly, and we reasonably expected that our messages were getting to the governor. We also could discuss the benefits and costs of agency decisions. But with Zipperer at the helm, we heard much more often that "the governor said" this or that, and the case was closed. I attributed this to Zipperer's seemingly mushy personality and his desire to avoid conflict. It's hard to nail a jellyfish to the wall.

Zipperer was a nice guy, but he didn't seem to want to engage in problem solving. He was content with just painting over festering issues. He was the kind of guy who would stand in front of a train wreck saying, "Nothing to see here. Move along." At the DOC, there was always a plethora of problems, and many of them involved getting input or permission from the governor's office before proceeding. That would become more than problematic with Rich as chief of staff and newly promoted Deputy Chief of Staff for Communications Jocelyn Webster at his side.

Zipperer took the unprecedented step of creating three more deputy chiefs of staff and implementing what I called the "three degrees of separation." Cabinet secretaries would no longer deal with the governor *or* the chief of staff, but instead were relegated to dealing with one of Rich's deputy minions, three levels away from the governor. It was clear to everyone in the cabinet that we were intentionally being kept as far from the governor as possible. He could not risk having the mud of state agency business splattering on his shiny presidential hopes.

The cabinet was obviously becoming aggravated, constantly dealing with cranky legislators. As we would meet with legislators, we expected the usual complaints about one issue or the other that involved some constituent or a pet project. However, we started hearing from legislators of both parties that they were unhappy with the governor's office. In fact, some Republican legislators had told secretaries that when they met with representatives of the governor's office, they were told, "The secretaries don't run these agencies, we do." This was especially galling coming from Rich's deputy chiefs of staff or their staff of "twenty-somethings" who acted very empowered.

While Walker's presidential campaign was stumbling along, his appearances in the debates were less than impressive. In fact, they were somewhat embarrassing. He was like a broken record trying to make his actions against labor unions in Wisconsin the centerpiece of why people should elect him. He seemed to lack a depth of understanding on the more relevant issues of the day. It felt like he was waving his hands trying to scream, "What about me? What about all that Act 10 stuff? I did big, bold reforms!" It wasn't getting the traction he had experienced at the outset. Maybe he was right: He peaked too early. In fact, his deep-pocket donors were already moving on, and Walker was watching his once-promising national political future fizzle like a Fourth of July sparkler at the end of its run.

Then came Trump. Walker tried to maintain his folksy Midwestern nice guy persona, but he had no clue how to handle a sausage grinder like Donald Trump. When Walker tried to stand up to Trump, Trump skewered him by saying Wisconsin was a state in decline, the citizens were polarized, and he had a monumental failure on his hands. Trump eviscerated Walker, and all he could do was stand there and stammer. Walker looked small and insignificant on the national stage, and his recently inflated ego with media attention was being deflated by the biggest windbag in the presidential campaign. Although I didn't think Walker deserved all the egg Trump threw on him, some of it was sticking. The spotlight on Scott Walker quickly moved away, and he was left standing in the dark with big bills to pay and wallets turned in another direction.

With Walker floundering on the national stage, Zipperer went to great lengths to distance the governor from his cabinet. The biweekly cabinet meetings suddenly slowed down to "as needed." He later took the step of breaking the cabinet up into "groups" to meet with, trying to avoid getting all the secretaries together where we could frankly say what was on our minds. My feeling was that Zipperer felt overwhelmed when he had that many people in one place willing to tell him what was wrong. It was easier to reduce the volume rather than change the station.

The secretaries were becoming increasingly frustrated with Zipperer and his method of fracturing the cabinet. Our separation from the governor was taking its toll. There were only a few secretaries who would speak their minds on issues independently, even if that involved telling the emperor he had no clothes. DOT Secretary Mark Gottlieb and I often spoke of our frustrations with the actions of the governor's office. We dared to speak truth to power in the cabinet meetings, and that was not a quality the Walker administration appreciated. They wanted cheerleaders and adoring fans, not linebackers or dirty uniforms. Time and again, Mark warned them of the impending transportation shortfalls, and I would warn about the impending DOC crisis du jour. Their reaction was to put it all off. This was a governor hell-bent on not raising taxes or seeking other funding sources because it might tarnish his story. Meanwhile, Wisconsin's roads and prison system continued to degrade just to defend a politician's mantra.

"One cannot speak truth to power, if power has no use for the truth"
James Rivington

Zipperer's deputy chief of staff for communication, Jocelyn Webster, had joined the Walker administration amid the Act 10 uproar, and some of the cabinet secretaries guessed she had been referred from the national GOP, as she was supposedly a protégé of Karl Rove. Webster was young, brash, outspoken, and could be obnoxious. She did not respect cabinet secretaries or the work we did. Her only concern was making the governor look good, and anything that rubbed up against that was considered the enemy. I wasted no time in telling Zipperer of the problems she was creating for my agency. Zipperer was not concerned, or at least he didn't seem to be. I think he was afraid of Webster because she had been sent from the national GOP, and Walker was flattered she had been sent to him. Supposedly, Walker and Webster were very close, and nobody dared to try and step between them.

Zipperer's inaction only emboldened Jocelyn. At one particular low point, she screamed at me during the Lincoln Hills investigation, "Your agency is out of control! What are you doing about it? Do you know what this is doing to the governor?" I didn't know if she was just ignorant about our repeated requests for the governor and his administration to engage with us to make changes, but she certainly seemed to be uninformed. She apparently wanted me to wave a magic wand and make everything better. She also never mentioned the fact that the governor neglected to tell me that he had been warned by a judge about problems at Lincoln Hills 10 months before I arrived. Now she was saying it was the DOC's fault for having to request the investigation even though Walker for three years had concealed that warning. Three years that the agency could have used in addressing that judge's concerns. I'm quite confident that Webster was proselytizing to the governor that I was the problem with Corrections and was likely advocating for my replacement in an effort to change the story.

It got to the point that our agency could not respond to *any* press inquiries whatsoever without her first reviewing and, in almost every case, rewriting our releases. Webster or one of her followers authored pretty much anything the DOC put out after June 2015.

I spoke with First Lady Tonette Walker in February 2016 at a meeting in my office shortly before I left the DOC, and she expressed her disdain for Webster in no uncertain terms. It was one thing for the cabinet secretaries to express frustration, but it was a far bigger issue if Tonette was out to end Webster's time with the governor. Tonette told me, "Mark my words, she will be gone soon." Sure enough, a few weeks after I left state government, Webster was gone. I liked Tonette. She did what she said she would do.

Walker was very loyal to his political donor base, and I believe he felt a need to prove that to them. Many times, throughout my tenure, we were told by the governor's office to meet with various private sector service providers and private prison operators. Eric Schutt had shared with me that when Walker was advocating for his tough-on-crime legislation, he was also very much in favor of contracting with private prison companies. Those private prison companies were also big campaign donors to candidates across the country.

During the presidential primaries and Walker's short-lived campaign, I was contacted by an executive from a private sector prison supply company. He explained they had been golfing in California with Walker the week before, and Walker urged them to reach out to me personally to see if there were any business opportunities. Out of respect, I took many of those meetings throughout my term. However, they did not usually translate into any business unless they could demonstrate they were the best and most affordable option. There was no way I was going to let political favors drag my agency or my integrity down the drain. I don't know if that contributed to my career ending at the DOC, but the thought was always in the back of my mind that it likely didn't help.

As the investigation into the Lincoln Hills issues continued, the distance between the governor's office and the DOC grew steadily. At one point in early September 2015, after the Lincoln Hills case had been in the paper nonstop for weeks, Chief of Staff Zipperer called to cancel my upcoming one-on-one meeting with the governor to discuss our agency budget issues. This was extremely concerning to me because one of the core issues he needed to understand was that budget issues were partly to blame for the problems at Lincoln Hills. But he could not get himself far enough away from the ringing alarm bells. Unfortunately, he didn't seem to understand that just because you moved farther away, didn't mean the fire was out.

For four consecutive budgets prior, including the two budgets I submitted to Walker, the DOC had requested funding for Lincoln Hills to add mental health positions, cameras for security, facility redesign, and more. Every single time, those requests were cut by the governor's office from the DOC budget submissions and never made it to the legislature for review. When I asked Zipperer why he was canceling my budget meeting with the governor, he replied, "We can't have you or the DOC anywhere near him right now." I understood the "right now" to be related to his struggling presidential bid and the Lincoln Hills issues.

Essentially, with the largest state budget for the largest cabinet agency, I would have no opportunity to inform the governor directly on critical issues we faced because of appearances while he was on the national stage. How did that serve the citizens of Wisconsin? Who was he working for? Ultimately, I would be the only secretary that would not have the opportunity to speak personally with the governor to advocate for my budget. It felt to me, and all of our executive staff, as if our agency was being punished for not staying out of the news—news that could have been tempered months before had the governor listened to our pleas for assistance and engaged.

We were very concerned by the position the governor's office was taking in leaving the DOC and Lincoln Hills out on an island and offering no support for a problem that was not going to disappear without considerable effort and resources. We were overcrowded, our staff was overworked to intolerable levels because of difficulties in hiring, and it was just a matter of time before something bad was going to happen.

We were so concerned, that I prepared a document called "DOC Vacancy and Pay Plan Issues." In it, I noted that "the DOC is presently about 270 inmates above our capacity." I wrote that we were "experiencing critical personnel vacancy issues within the security ranks," and that "wages for the security classifications are well behind what counties and surrounding states are paying." I urged that their wages be increased to at least be somewhat competitive with county jails to help us alleviate the shortages. I proposed modernizing our buildings, which would "save the state approximately $430 million over the next 15 years." And I was blunt about the potential risks: "The climate in the institutions is extremely divisive with the number of vacancies currently faced in some institutions. History shows us that fatigued staff mixed with angry inmates can spark an uprising with tremendous costs, both fiscally and physically."

My concern was that the governor's office would feign ignorance of the many challenges that the DOC faced and then later blame me for not communicating those problems to them. This was based on their militant insistence on not creating or maintaining records. No records, no proof. Their insistence on insulating the governor's office from any potential exposure was more than a distraction; it was infuriating for me and others in the cabinet. It was no way to solve problems and only served to give the governor deniability. Unfortunately, I knew that preparing a document that outlined agency problems and the need for the governor to engage would not be well received. But it had to be done.

I printed that document, which I still have a copy of, and placed three copies in a sealed envelope: one for the governor, one for Zipperer, and one for DOA Secretary Scott Neitzel. In mid-October 2015, my staff and I were meeting with the governor's staff regarding our budget papers for submission to the governor because the governor would not meet with us personally. I walked over with my deputy secretary to Zipperer and Neitzel, who were standing together. My deputy secretary had no idea what was in the envelope when I handed it to Zipperer, but I wanted a witness there in case they would claim they never received it. I simply said, "There's a document in here that you should review. I made three copies. One for each of you, and one for the governor."

Zipperer immediately became uncomfortable as I put the envelope into his hands, and he glanced around to see who was looking. I told him that I didn't want to send it electronically, being sensitive to his disdain for records. I often wondered if he treated that document as an open record since I handed it to him acting in my role as a cabinet secretary in the governor's conference room. Perhaps someone in the press would make that inquiry someday—and then remember how Walker and Schimel would eventually go after me.

The issues surrounding Lincoln Hills were now in the paper just about every day. Although I was often mentioned, it was quickly turning into "Scott Walker's DOC." That was not a positive thing for him, even though he and his staff continued to ignore our pleas for help. It was also apparent to me that it would not be good for my tenure at the DOC, even though there was nothing I could do to change the lack of assistance from the governor's office or quicken the pace of the DOJ's pitiful investigation.

My calls for help to the governor's office were persistent. We needed additional pay for officers and other DOC staff positions so we could attract candidates to jobs that most people would not want. We needed more mental health resources. We needed more medical staff. We couldn't keep teachers and needed incentives. We needed more prison space. Those requests fell on deaf ears, and I would be told by an insider in the governor's office later that my persistence in advocating for pay increases was one of the primary reasons I needed to leave my cabinet post. This was not what cabinet secretaries for a conservative zealot like Walker should be doing. Giving money to corrections or state employees wouldn't get him any votes or win his appreciation.

When I expressed my concerns to Zipperer on many occasions concerning the pay inequity problems, he would just nod with a look of apathy on his face. We had warned Rich and his deputies continually that we were on the brink of disaster with overcrowding, staff shortages, and, in particular, the problems at Lincoln Hills. Rich's message was consistent: Put another coat of paint on it. In other words, we don't want you to fix problems; just wear a happy face and deny problems exist.

That was probably at the core of the consternation that I had with the governor's staff and they had with me. You don't take a person whose entire life has been focused on fixing problems and tell them to "put a coat of paint on it." Problems don't often fix themselves, and I could not abide by the notion that we should deny those problems and tell everyone things were grand while my staff and the inmates were at incredible risk of injury or death.

The problem with Walker and some of his appointees is that they think the only judgment that matters is what the press will say. That's because they don't go and see staff members in the hospital who were attacked by an inmate. They don't have to deal with staff suicides and try to understand the impact that has on lives. They don't have to hold grieving family members in their arms who lost their children.

You see, Walker didn't have to go from institution to institution and talk with state employees who were already making subpar wages while having to figure out how to work around a 12 percent income cut that he had delivered to them in Act 10. In fact, he made a point of staying away from all things related to my agency. When you are being driven around in your plush Chevy Suburban and enjoying the exceptional cooking capabilities of the executive residence chef, it's hard to feel the consequences of your policies. And when you are on the phone with the Koch brothers or Sheldon Adelson begging for campaign contributions, you can't be distracted by the reality that your employees are trying to figure out how to pay their bills or losing their homes.

One of the issues our agency repeatedly brought before the governor and his staff was our overcrowding. That overcrowding was a direct result of legislation passed in the 1990s under the guise of being "tough on crime." That legislation was written by Scott Walker when he was a legislator, and the last thing he or his staff wanted to hear was that this was now a detriment to the state. When I spoke with Zipperer on that very point, he looked at me with a smirk and said, "The governor wrote that legislation. Do you think he wants to hear that it is now the source of your problems while he is campaigning for president?" That was a not-so-veiled way of saying, "Shut up and take your concerns back to your office."

In hindsight, I think that the governor's office thought that being a lifelong cop, I would be strongly in favor of the tough-on-crime stance the governor had staked out years before. And, before going into the DOC, I was. What the governor and his staff did not understand was that once you take over the DOC and have to face the realities and the consequences of prison populations, aging inmates, mental health treatment, addiction programming, skills training, segregation reform, and any number of other competing challenges that affect recidivism, your position changes. Your level of understanding changes. Your vision changes and, ultimately, your direction changes.

That transformation had the potential to place corrections leaders at odds with the governor, and the sad reality was that DOC leaders were replaceable with people who would share the governor's vision and ignore the facts. I just was not one of them. An interesting statistic I learned in new secretary school was that the average tenure for a DOC agency head was about 24 months. I suspect it took that long to understand your job, become informed about the challenges, and try to address them with your governor. The result was that you would either leave because they wouldn't work with you, or they would replace you with someone else who ostensibly agreed with them. Kill the messenger, hide the corpse, and move on.

Zipperer had my team meet on a regular basis with Deputy Chief of Staff for Operations Matt Moroney. Moroney had come from a political background, and he had a way about him that made many people uncomfortable. He would listen to you with his head cocked a little to one side with a smirk on his face that was difficult to read. He earned the nickname "The Smarmy One" from my staff, and we never felt he was in our corner.

Time and time again, we would bring documents to our meetings to discuss the challenges the agency was facing. Often, Moroney would push documents back across his desk to us saying there was no need to have them laying around in the governor's office. My staff saw this as yet another avenue of deniability for a governor's office that wanted to micromanage our operations without leaving a fingerprint at the scene of the carnage.

Considering the overcrowding issue and ongoing problems with Lincoln Hills, I began to wonder whether we should reopen the Ethan Allen juvenile facility, which was sitting empty near Milwaukee. So, I went over by myself in March 2015 to see Ethan Allen and get a feel for its potential utility. What I found surprised me.

The institution was in pretty good shape. It had some expensive work done shortly before it was closed and certainly looked like it could be viable. When I returned to the DOC, I made some inquiries on the ability to reopen it as a mechanism to address our burgeoning population problems. The administrator of Management Services explained that might not be a popular idea since it was Walker who closed it in the first place. Regardless, I asked for someone to give me a rough idea of what it would cost to put the institution back online. Management Services thought it would be roughly $5 million at that time to remediate the mold and lead paint issues and get it open.

There were many who backed Walker's move to close Ethan Allen, citing the mold issue and lead paint concerns. In reality, the maintenance supervisor at Ethan Allen told me that those issues were pretty much confined. He also pointed out that the extent of those problems would have been limited had the governor's office not directed the heat be turned off in the buildings after the facility was shut down to save on heating costs. That decision left pipes to burst and a very expensive mess to clean up.

Throughout the summer of 2015, I began sketching out some ideas on utilizing Ethan Allen and finding better ways to address the juvenile corrections issues before us. I had been speaking with former Governor Tommy Thompson regarding ideas we shared on improving training and job skill development for inmates transitioning to release. Tommy was an excellent example of a governor who could change his perspective based on facts and education. He was the governor who built the Supermax Correctional Institution during the tough-on-crime days, but he was also educated on the self-licking ice cream cone of corrections. Tommy became an enthusiastic supporter of the DOC and was forward-leaning with his ideas. I wish Walker had been so interested.

I enjoyed working and speaking with Tommy Thompson. I still recall the irritation the governor's office had with Tommy over the charity livestock auction at the State Fair. Tommy and Walker were both to be celebrity auctioneers at the event, and Tommy did what he did best. He worked the crowd, got people involved, and made it fun for everyone involved. Walker, on the other hand, didn't have the same level of gravitas that Tommy could deliver. The governor's office was angry that Tommy had "upstaged" Walker, and they said they wouldn't have the two of them together in public again. Bad contrast, I guess.

I remember talking with Tommy one time when it was just the two of us, and I asked him what he thought of Governor Walker and Act 10. I won't repeat the colorful observations he made, but suffice to say he did not care much for either. He went on to explain that you can't lead as governor and bulldoze over the other party. His view on Act 10 was that it was a mistake, and he didn't like the way it was handled. Tommy was the most successful governor Wisconsin ever had in many respects, and a large part of that success was due to his ability to work toward consensus, something that Walker could learn from.

There were many good ideas on how to deal with juvenile corrections across the country. In Wisconsin, we had pioneered some of them, such as the "Grow Academy," which was a small institution for juveniles just outside of Madison. The focus was on teaching kids' agricultural skills and business planning. The goal was not to teach them to be farmers but to develop life skills every adult would need, including patience, focus, planning, and execution.

There were also some very engaged legislators on corrections issues, including Senators Jon Erpenbach, Rick Gudex, Jennifer Shilling, Lena Taylor, and Van Wanggaard, and Representatives Evan Goyke, Gordon Hintz, Rob Hutton, Amy Loudenbeck, John Nygren, and Michael Schraa. I discussed many different ideas that we had for addressing juvenile and adult corrections with all of them; some welcomed it, while others were more skeptical. But at least they cared enough to engage, which was more than I could say about the governor's office.

We brought different plans to the governor's office to address the Lincoln Hills issues. My first plan was to reopen Ethan Allen as a youth institution as it had been previously, albeit with more staff and mental health services. That would bring most of the youth closer to home and their support systems. We would then convert Lincoln Hills into a minimum-security adult institution that would become more of a technical college facility for inmates transitioning to release, where we could focus on training, skills building, substance abuse counseling, and education to help improve their chances of not ending up back in prison.

The northern part of the state has minimum security correctional camps, which then could be converted into a few regional youth facilities when the adult population was transferred to Lincoln Hills. That would give the youth from the north country, or youth that preferred to be away from Milwaukee, a more reformative experience in a quiet setting with smaller populations.

The second idea was to convert Ethan Allen into the technical college for adult inmates since so many of our inmates came from the Milwaukee area. That would put them near businesses that might hire them and make interviewing and support mechanisms more readily available. We would then convert Lincoln Hills into a minimum-security adult institution and transition the minimum-security adult camps into youth facilities and work with Milwaukee County in building a dedicated facility for their youth.

Additionally, there was one program in the state of Missouri that I was particularly interested in pursuing. It used a model that focused on keeping youth closer to home in smaller, more personal correctional facilities. It was the same plan that had caught the attention of Representative Goyke. I wanted that type of effort to be done in conjunction with Milwaukee County officials so that both agencies would be invested in the outcomes. In my mind, there was too much of the "us and them" attitude between the state and county juvenile correction issues that needed to be addressed.

I spoke with Zipperer about these ideas shortly after he came into office as chief of staff in September 2015. Rich seemed underwhelmed with the ideas and mentioned that he thought some developer was interested in the Ethan Allen property. Additionally, he said there was no way that building a facility for Milwaukee would fly with the governor or the legislators. He said that if Milwaukee wanted their own facility, they could build it and pay for it. Ultimately, I drafted an outline of the ideas and gave them to Deputy Chief of Staff Matt Moroney during our one-on-one meeting. He did not seem impressed with the ideas either. I was disappointed with the response, but it was indicative of an administration that refused to try and solve Corrections' problems when it was easier to ignore them and move on.

In an effort to address our hiring shortages, we offered several different pay plan options, which Moroney also waved off. He lectured us at one point that we needed to stop advocating for pay increases and instead take a hard stand like he did when he was the deputy secretary of the DNR.

He described proudly how he "stood up" to the DNR wardens when they were demanding pay increases and told them they were only getting a small percentage. He then took credit for them backing down, claiming his actions saved the state money. I sat quietly for a moment and said to him, "That's all very nice, Matt, but there is no comparison to be made between your circumstances and ours." He seemed shocked and insisted there was. I then explained to him that DNR wardens are a few hundred employees at best, while my uniformed ranks alone were well over five thousand.

Additionally, I pointed out that DNR wardens worked both outside and in normal office atmospheres, where they interacted with people who did not typically wish to harm them or throw feces or urine on them. It was difficult to compare Corrections officers working in difficult surroundings with DNR wardens who had their state-issued vehicles, their state-issued boat, their state-issued snowmobile, and their state-issued ATV driving around our beautiful state. Lastly, I pointed out that the DNR wardens started at a higher rate of pay than my senior uniformed officers were making after a decade of service. Nonetheless, he said I needed to follow his lead because they would not approve our pay plans.

My frustration was building with an administration that seemed, nearly five years after Act 10, to still be at war with state employees. We pulled our budget people together and started sifting through every single available dollar to try and come up with money to do a pay incentive. Finally, we calculated that we had enough to offer an across-the-board raise of $1 per hour to uniformed staff. Moroney dismissed it as too much. He obviously had taken a page from the governor's handbook on no negotiation. He was willing to let the DOC continue to slide into the chasm that had been created by a current breed of politicians whose only interest was cutting budgets in order to chase conservative votes. I often wished that each one of those politicians could be forced to work just one month in the prisons so that they could appreciate what they were doing to an already challenging work environment.

Ultimately, when my replacement came in after me, he would only be allowed to offer 80 cents an hour; obviously Moroney had his way. I wondered how Moroney would survive on a corrections officer's pay and could only imagine his reaction to having feces or urine thrown on him. That picture still makes me smile.

In the midst of the ongoing budget problems and our efforts to try and figure out what the DOJ had been doing for 10 months with the Lincoln Hills investigation, the governor dropped his presidential bid and came limping back to Wisconsin, bloodied by a bombastic candidate who would eventually become our president. The governor made news by withdrawing from the race with great fanfare, pointing to the need for the party to come together and essentially push Trump off to the sidelines. The governor was mad, he was belittled, his limelight had dimmed, and like many others, he feared what Trump could do to this country if elected.

I happened to see Walker two days after he dropped out of the race and came back to the capitol. I was in his office for another meeting, and we had a few private moments to talk. I told him that I was sorry his presidential campaign didn't work out the way he had hoped but was happy to see him back so we could work on the many problems facing our agency. He looked exhausted and commented on how destructive the discourse had become with Trump in the fray, and he worried about the election. He made it clear what he thought about Trump and feared that he would destroy the Republican Party. I respected his apparent position of principle, but that was washed away when, as the months went by, I watched him prostitute himself to the same bully that had wasted no time in ripping his dignity away in front of the nation. Trump had humiliated Walker, making him look so small and insignificant, yet Walker rolled over like a dog wanting his belly scratched and became what I feared he might be— shameless and unprincipled.

When Walker returned to the state, he wasted little time in calling a secretary-only cabinet meeting at the capitol after work one evening. There was a fear I sensed in this once-confident governor during that meeting. Gone was the self-assured guy who only weeks before had his party fawning over him. He looked like a guy who was worried he was about to lose his job. There was a sense of urgency in the room. They brought in pizza, and we openly addressed the 800-pound GOP elephant in the room. The governor's absence to chase after his presidential ambitions had cost him dearly in the polls in Wisconsin. Many of the legislators were angry with him and were now openly defying him as they sensed his vulnerability. He wanted us to help him plot a path back to popularity. My deepest fear was that he and his party, desperate to hold onto the governorship and legislature, would plan some other big, bold plan that would further cast the state into chaos. Because, in chaos there is opportunity, and Walker had learned to feed on that. He was the chaos candidate.

There were many ideas thrown around the room, and I finally spoke up and said, "Governor, your strength is in talking with people one-on-one. I think you need to come down off the podium and get out to meet people again. Do a traveling road show of town hall meetings across the state and get public about it." It was the same strategy I had used in the DOC. The governor apparently liked the idea, and then the rest of the cabinet started chiming in on how that could be done when they saw his interest. They encouraged him to bring along different secretaries, depending on the issues in the community that might be affected by our presence.

The plans were put together and would soon be in the news. It all looked very positive until it became apparent that the audiences would include invited guests only and not the public. The administration's fear of a protestor spectacle at every stop would eventually turn the town hall meetings into little more than paid infomercial dog and pony shows for future campaign ads. And, not surprisingly, the DOC secretary was never invited along to any of those town hall meetings. "Nothing good comes out of Corrections." 🦫

THE SCHIMEL SHUFFLE

The DOJ would try and lead the press and others to believe that their efforts surrounding the Lincoln Hills investigation were adequate. In fact, as I write this book, they still try to maintain that facade. But after information was shared with the press concerning the fact that the DOJ only had one agent working on the case part-time for over 10 months, Schimel was asked if he should have devoted more resources to Lincoln Hills, to which he arrogantly answered, "Yeah. Hindsight's 20/20."

The only problem with Schimel's quip was that hindsight had nothing to do with their response. Time and time again, I had underlined the urgency of this case to him, but he never seemed to take it seriously. Either that or he was intentionally trying to downplay the case at someone's direction. That concern kept coming back to me. We put a ton of attention and effort into Lincoln Hills while I was secretary. There was nobody at the DOC sitting on their hands or wasting time, while the DOJ agents stopped by irregularly to do an interview here and there.

Interestingly, Schimel would comment to the press over two years later in December 2017 that I should have done more about Lincoln Hills, and saying that I was a "failed" secretary. Blame shifting is not a new concept to Schimel. As I write this book, the attorney general continues to hide behind the "We don't comment on open investigations" facade. The man who would end my career citing open records issues and who boasts about his dedication to transparency hides behind open records that don't make him look good, like a child behind his mother's skirt. Interesting for the man who later attempted to avoid the open records law by specifically instructing his staff to hide the details of his paid appearance at a national conference with a concerning agenda.

About this same frantic time, Zipperer called and advised that he was going to draft a letter to me, instructing me to take actions to address the Lincoln Hills issues. My staff and I were dumbfounded. This was the guy who had done everything possible to avoid getting involved with the Lincoln Hills issues. He was going to now write me a letter that would undoubtedly look like the governor's office was galloping in to take control of the situation that they went out of their way to avoid—a situation they had exacerbated by refusing to engage on.

Zipperer asked me to come to the capitol to help he and Moroney draft the letter he was going to send me. No exchange of drafts by email, but just come down here and do it in person. He didn't want to have a record trail showing that this whole exercise was merely a public record charade. Once again, I was dragged downtown to avoid the creation of a public record.

When I arrived, I again expressed my concern that the administration and the legislature needed to address the situation at Lincoln Hills through action and funding, not just exchanging emails and letters. And once again, Zipperer told me that there was no intention of dedicating funds to fix the problem. I asked what it would take to get someone to take the problems seriously, and he simply said, "A lawsuit." I asked what he meant, and he said that the legislature had a well-known tendency to respond to lawsuits rather than acting preemptively. My response was, "So, we have to pay millions of dollars in lawsuit costs before we can expect anything to happen?" And he just looked at me nodding. These people were maddening.

We ultimately drafted the letter, and Zipperer said he would email it to me, explaining that it would then be creating a record that he could release promptly to the press demonstrating the governor's leadership on this critical issue. It made me want to vomit. Zipperer then instructed me to draft a response letter outlining what we had done in the DOC to respond to the governor's instructions. When I had the draft completed, I was to call Zipperer on the phone and read it to him. When it was approved, I would then send it by email to create another record the governor's office would promptly release, demonstrating his command of the situation. All of this for the governor who refused to even visit the institution or talk to us about our budget needs. Shameful.

After the letter exchange and repeated requests for assistance in getting funding for much-needed security enhancements, they finally had me meet with DOA Secretary Scott Neitzel to discuss some funding options. Not because they necessarily thought they should, but because the media attention was getting more intense by the day. Essentially, the answer was, "You have to fund it out of your own budget, but we will help find a way to move the money around." In other words, rearranging the deck chairs on the Titanic. Unfortunately, that wasn't very helpful but certainly maintained the optics that the governor wouldn't put any extra funds into Corrections.

We couldn't wait any longer for Walker and his obstructionist staff to help with solutions, so I instructed that the Division of Juvenile Corrections to begin installing cameras in the areas identified as blind spots in previous budget requests and during the investigation.

Additionally, I instructed that body cameras be purchased for all officers working on the housing units at Lincoln Hills. There was such a clamoring by youth claiming they were being tortured and injured that I felt we had to protect the officers from false accusations and the youth from anyone who might consider harming them, including other youth. At my direction, we had already done a year-long test of body cameras at Waupun Correctional Institution and found they had great benefits. We wasted no time in pulling the trigger and getting them ordered. It was time to take definitive action and stop hoping the governor would help us.

We also determined that training had been identified as one of the primary problems, and we moved quickly to make immediate changes to new youth counselor training. All these things were positive moves, but unfortunately, the union folks continued to fan the flames with the staff. Their unrelenting anger over Act 10 and the unwillingness by some senior staff to accept the evolving treatment of incarcerated youth led them to feed negative stories to the media, especially the *Milwaukee Journal Sentinel*. The DOC was strictly forbidden by the governor's office from responding to accusations made by the staff, the union, or the newspaper, which only exacerbated the problem. We were left to burn.

It was frustrating to watch the staff sing the chorus of "this is because of Act 10." I didn't disagree with them that Act 10 had impacted our abilities to hire and maintain staff, but it seemed so shortsighted to try and wave that flag as the media focused their spotlight on the problems at the institution. The constant shouting about Act 10 only further reinforced the governor and legislature's aversion to getting involved with the problems we were dealing with. The staff was too blind to see that their actions could well assure that their place of employment could be shut down. And their union just seemed to pile it on, oblivious to the negative effects on the legislators who might have helped them. They were changing the story from bad things staff did into a union battle. That would get them sympathy from some Democrats but only push away most Republicans who had already hitched their wagon to Act 10.

Then one late Friday afternoon, in early November 2015, I received an unannounced conference call from DOJ Senior Counsel Paul Connell, DCI Administrator Dave Matthews, and Assistant Attorney General Chris Liegel. It was one of the strangest calls I had ever received. Connell announced that they wished to advise the DOC that they had determined a "culture" existed at Lincoln Hills that they felt created a danger for the youth being held there. Then, they also advised that pursuant to state law, they had notified the Lincoln County Sheriff that they felt youth were at risk in our institution.

I was beyond shocked that somehow they had investigated for over 10 months, supposedly ran a John Doe investigation, and while they did not have enough information to arrest a single person, they were now indicting a "culture" at Lincoln Hills. I told them that I would be on my way to the DOJ momentarily and we would discuss this in person. It was outrageous that the DOJ would now make a blanket statement about a "culture" at Lincoln Hills as the explanation for why their department hadn't done anything yet. It was easy to cover their inaction by blaming something so vague as a "culture." It was just a red herring to try and make a murky claim that something bigger was lurking just beyond the fog they had created. At least that was the way it would be sold to the press, who took it and ran. It was nothing more than a DOJ diversion. It became known to some of us as the Schimel Shuffle, and I suspected it was being done to get the case out of their hands before someone realized what a mess they had made.

My deputy secretary and legal chief came with me, and the DOJ again repeated their feeling about a "culture" and how they had contacted the sheriff. We were incredulous at the actions they had arbitrarily taken without even speaking to me, the governor's office, or apparently anyone else as they tried to get the Lincoln Hills hot potato out of their laps. When I questioned why they did not call us first, they dug in their heels and simply said they "did what they felt they had to do." We were furious. This was the same leadership team at the DOJ that dawdled for months with a part-time investigation we felt merited much more effort than they were able to muster, and now they decided to hit the panic button without speaking with us.

I asked why they felt they needed to contact the sheriff's office, and Matthews said it was his statutory responsibility that once he became aware that children were at risk, the notification needed to be made. I explained to Matthews and Connell that I fully understood the mandatory reporting laws, and that was exactly why *I had notified the sheriff almost a year before* and requested that DOC be allowed to refer the case to DCI as the law enforcement agency to investigate. I explained that *they* had been notified and that's why *we* had requested the investigation. It seemed now that they were taking the position that they weren't the responsible law enforcement agency after the pitiful effort they had put into a case they were just now realizing was very serious. What was the meaning of their sworn oath, their badges, their guns, their statewide jurisdiction? What was the attorney general, who is supposed to be the top law enforcement official in the state?

Assistant Attorney General Chris Liegel, the prosecutor for the investigation, stated at that meeting that he disagreed with the decision by DOJ to call the sheriff, which was a gutsy proclamation of truth in that meeting with his supervisor present. Connell looked annoyed at the comment, and Matthews stuck his chin out saying, "We stand behind the decision," making it clear that he and Connell were the ones to initiate the call and raise the stakes on Lincoln Hills.

We immediately suspected that Connell and Matthews were trying to throw a Hail Mary to shift responsibility to someone else. Why? Because it was quickly becoming obvious through the press that the DOC was expending millions of dollars trying to respond to unknown facts the DOJ refused to share with us in our efforts to lean forward and be proactive. They knew that the spotlight would swing to them, and they wanted that light pointed somewhere else. Connell and Matthews had the most to lose if their lack of effort became public; they were the ones charged with overseeing the investigation. Their scapegoat was obviously going to be me and the DOC.

To be clear, the DOJ's failures on the Lincoln Hills investigation were, from our standpoint, purely management-based: from DCI Administrator Dave Matthews to Senior Counsel Paul Connell and finally Attorney General Brad Schimel, because he is ultimately responsible for what his agency does, or doesn't do, as was the case here.

The special agents and civilian staff with the DCI do exactly what they are told by their bosses, and that was apparently not a lot. It was the upper management, led by Connell, who was responsible for overseeing the DCI, that made the determination that the case did not warrant the amount of investigative resources the DOC felt it did. The decision to treat the investigation so offhandedly was not the agents' to make. This was a monumental failure of leadership that placed youth at continued risk while DOJ management repeatedly put the case on the back burner and stonewalled our efforts.

At that meeting, I insisted that we call Lincoln County Sheriff Jeff Yeager to discuss the DOJ's notification to him about the "culture" at Lincoln Hills. When we did call the sheriff, Jeff expressed his concern about why the DOJ thought they should be notifying him. He agreed with my position that the requirement to notify him had already occurred when the DOC had called him months before and requested that we be allowed to take the case to the DOJ. Like us, he felt that this had been the DOJ's responsibility since they were notified back in January.

In speaking with Jeff after that call, he and I agreed that it appeared the DOJ was trying to shift responsibility from its own failed investigation into someone else's lap. Throughout that meeting, I could tell by Connell's face that he was worried about what was coming. He could also not hide his loathing for every word I spoke that insinuated that he might own some of the blame for what was happening with the DOJ's failed investigation. The buck stopped at his desk since he was the person overseeing the DCI and would be the direct conduit to Schimel. Connell had been quick to proudly tell multiple police chiefs and sheriffs who contacted me that he was the man responsible for the oversight of the DCI. However, when the results of his failed leadership were revealed, he, like the attorney general, claimed that he wasn't up to speed on the case as they backed away with their hands in the air.

We notified the governor's office about what the DOJ had elected to do, and Rich Zipperer was none too happy. I had warned Rich many times before that the DOJ was mishandling the investigation, and he was repeatedly reluctant to engage them. Now I took the opportunity to remind him that I had explained to him repeatedly that the DOJ had no concern for our agency or the governor's exposure. He told me that we needed to meet with the DOJ and find out what their investigation had uncovered since they were trying to back away with no findings except something vague about the culture at Lincoln Hills.

My legal chief was very concerned with the avenue the DOJ was taking, and he clearly understood that they were looking to hang blame on anyone they could to cover up their investigation errors. I sent a terse email to Connell, copying his attorneys, my legal chief, and my deputy secretary, outlining my grave concerns with the way they had handled the case and their late-in-the-game efforts to take some kind of action.

The next morning, I was called to the capitol by Zipperer and Moroney, where they chastised me for sending that email. They were obviously irritated that I had broken the cardinal rule of record avoidance. I wonder these days if that was the beginning of the end, because I had dared to create a record.

Subsequently, we sent a request, or more of a demand, that the DOJ come brief the DOC on their investigation. I invited Zipperer to join us at the meeting, and he declined. I was not surprised, because that might erase some of the deniability they had tried so hard to maintain. That meeting was held on November 19, 2015, in the secretary's conference room at the DOC. The DOJ sent Senior Counsel Paul Connell, Legal Services Administrator Dave Meaney, DCI Administrator Dave Matthews, DCI Regional Director Jody Wormet, DCI Special Agent in Charge Cindy Giese, and Assistant

Attorney General Chris Liegel. Interestingly, the agent who had been investigating the case part-time did not come. We were convinced that this was by design so that we could not ask him questions concerning what we were about to see.

The secretary's conference room table is about 18 feet long and seats 16 people. The DOJ rolled out an enormous timeline that extended from one end of the table to the other. Chris Liegel cautioned us that we could not take any photographs of any work they were presenting, and they would not supply us with any documents whatsoever with the excuse that their investigation was in progress and that there was an ongoing John Doe investigation. This was the same investigation they had told us in August was completed and moving to the prosecution phase—the same case Matthews told me was in a John Doe investigation back in May, six months earlier.

Chris then began his explanation of the investigation by saying they had found some very troubling things, including the fact that five youths had suffered broken bones as a result of their handling by officers.

I stopped Chris right there and said, "Chris, I believe there were three youths who suffered broken bones."

He immediately corrected me and said, "No, five."

I turned to my staff and said, "Are there three or five?"

My juvenile corrections administrator replied, "There were three, sir."

I then turned back to Chris and asked what should have been an obvious question: "Chris, you do have the medical records for each of these youths, don't you?" There was a palpable tension in the room and a troubling pause before he advised they did not have any medical records. We sat there in stunned silence, and I just stared at him, then Paul Connell, then Dave Matthews.

After a long uncomfortable pause, Chris said, "We found in several interviews that their statements seemed credible." My staff and I were thunderstruck. I explained that 100 percent of the females and about 85 percent of the males had diagnosed severe mental health issues and asked if they had considered that when evaluating the statements. He repeated that they found some of them credible.

I paused again, looking at my staff on one side of the table and then back at Chris before saying, "Please tell me you at least have the incident reports concerning the circumstances surrounding the injuries."

Again, the tension was palpable as he replied quietly, "We do not."

I pushed back from my position at the head of the table and looked around the room. Connell, sensing the exchange that was coming, rose and stated that he had to go to another meeting and beat feet out the door like a scared rabbit. I thought to myself, as he ran away, that he is not a guy I would want to work with because he runs at the first sign of conflict and lets others take the hits.

The rest of the DOJ staff sat there in silence. I finally said, "I find it incredible that in your investigation you have not taken the most basic and rudimentary steps of reviewing records surrounding the incidents involved. This is not just an oversight; it is a complete failure of basic investigative functions. Did it ever occur to anyone that the youth whom you found fully credible without any supporting documentation want to see the institution closed?" I added, "I am absolutely stunned that after more than 10 months of investigation, the DOJ has drawn conclusions and leveled damning accusations that are based on supposition, one-sided interviews, a lack of documentation, and completely lacking in any depth of understanding as to the circumstances surrounding the injuries."

There was a fair amount of stammering, looking at the ceiling, nervous glances, and attempts to try and explain away their sophomoric attempt to properly investigate something so serious as youth being potentially harmed by state employees. I then asked the closing question: "After all of this investigation over 10 months, do you have enough information or evidence to charge a single person with a crime?"

After another uncomfortable pause, Chris answered, "Not at this time, no." No wonder Connell ran like a gazelle when he saw the writing on the wall. My staff and I knew right then and there that the DOJ was going to do everything they could to get rid of this case and cast aspersions on us to distract the media.

I spoke with DOJ Legal Services Administrator Dave Meaney after the meeting and voiced my concerns with what had just happened. He stood stoically as I recited the errors of the investigation and the effects they would have on our agency and the exposure the governor would have due to their lack of effort. As we had suspected from the beginning, this investigation was nothing short of a halfhearted effort right up until they realized they had nothing to prosecute after the state had spent so much trying to blindly address concerns that they refused to inform us about. Then, their reaction was to wave their hands, call attention to the problem like it just manifested itself recently, and throw their agency into reverse thrust to escape the coming scrutiny. And that, my friends, is where they would have liked the story to end.

However, in the words of one of my favorite historical figures, Winston Churchill, "Now this is not the end. It is not even the beginning of the end. But it is, perhaps, the end of the beginning." ❧

THE SCHIMEL SHUFFLE

CYA

As the DOC prepared for the press backlash that would follow the DOJ's frantic attempts to backpedal from the investigation, we were also looking for other options to offer the governor's office on how to address the Lincoln Hills issues. They had already shunned the idea of closing the facility and moving to the Missouri Model, which I and, more recently, Representative Goyke had been in favor of. But he was a Democrat, so that wouldn't fly.

There was plenty of blame to go around. Were there employees at Lincoln Hills who did things they shouldn't have? Absolutely, and we removed them from duty as soon as we learned what they were accused of. But you cannot blame training issues when staff members do something so crazy as to decide to run "fight clubs" with incarcerated youth. You cannot blame management when an employee decides to open a locked box and destroy youth complaints to avoid getting in trouble. By the same token, as the law enforcement agency in charge of the investigation, you cannot shirk responsibility for conducting a thorough investigation to protect the innocent and bring charges against those who did wrong.

For instance, in the case of the officer who had "degloved" the youth's toes, we sent the video to the DOJ. We immediately relieved the officer of duty and placed him on administrative leave. He would resign a short time later.

After not hearing anything from the DOJ for a few days, I called DCI Administrator Dave Matthews and asked if he had the opportunity to review the video, and he said that he had. I told him that it was my impression that the officer had committed an assault, and he made no statement to agree or disagree. I then asked if the DOJ intended to make an arrest regarding that assault, and he replied that he didn't know what they would be doing and that he would leave the decision to the assistant attorney general handling the case. I told Matthews again that it was a clear the toes in the door were accidental, but yanking the tether strap and slamming the youth into the door was an assault. I encouraged them to file charges against the officer so that people could see we were serious about this case. No action was ever taken. Why? I'm convinced they were looking for a clean break from the case and didn't want any lingering charges with their name on them. They had abandoned their responsibility.

When I called Chief of Staff Rich Zipperer to advise him of the incident, he instructed me to come to the capitol and meet with him. When I arrived, I found Rich and Deputy Chief of Staff Matt Moroney waiting for me. When I closed the door and took my seat, I could see Rich was worked up. By this time, we had about 15 people out on paid administrative leave as a result of accusations made by youth that needed to be investigated. But we had no idea what the status was with these staff members regarding the DOJ investigation.

Rich looked at me, his face flush red, and said, "Fire them! Fire them all!"

I was stunned. I asked, "What do you mean?"

He repeated "I said, fire all of them." I tried to point out that these people had rights as state employees, and he said, "I don't care. Let them fight to get their jobs back. We have to do something to end this mess. The governor is taking all the heat."

I just shook my head and looked down at the floor. Moroney then chimed in that he would arrange to have a Department of Administration attorney assigned to assist us in terminating the staff since they were the mother ship of human resources for the state agencies.

I left the office completely demoralized. These politicians had absolutely no compunction about destroying lives to serve their purposes. It didn't matter if there was no just cause or any due process. It was all about changing the story no matter the cost because the governor was taking the heat. Unfortunately, leaders have to take the heat sometimes. Unless, of course, you are the governor: Then you have others do that for you and leave a trail of devastation and shattered lives in your rearview mirror.

I went back to meet with my executive staff and our human resource director to relay the orders I was given. They were equally as shocked, and we had some very animated discussions about how wrong this was and what would happen when we lost the appeals. Fortunately, we never came to that point. The DOA attorney who was assigned to assist us made the determination that the DOC could not just fire the staff members, absent just cause and due process. They delivered that message to their secretary, who in turn advised Zipperer. He was not happy. Politicians never like it when their plans get disrupted by such inconvenient things as rules, regulations, or laws. I couldn't help but wonder if Zipperer and Walker wished they had engaged with DOJ months earlier like we had been asking. Unfortunately, I would find out soon that their disdain for just cause and due process was more than a passing coincidence; it was methodology.

As this was all unfolding, the DOC Juvenile Corrections administrator, Paul Westerhaus, and the Lincoln Hills superintendent, John Ourada, both decided that they would retire. The writing was on the wall that a herd of scapegoats would be needed to distance the governor and the attorney general from any blame. They both agreed that for the agency to move forward, it would be best for them to step aside to allow for a new management team to come in and make changes.

Much was made in the press because I had positive words to say about both of them in their retirement announcement to the department. The fact was after almost a year into its investigation, the DOJ had no information whatsoever that these faithful public servants had done anything wrong. Before I announced their retirements, I specifically had our staff confirm with the DOJ that there was no information that implicated either of them in any regard, and that was affirmed. Paul and John were good men who devoted their lives to trying to help others, yet the press would try and make them out as under suspicion and me looking like a conspirator because I wouldn't just fire them without cause. As leaders, we are all judged in perfect hindsight by those that never had to deal with the issues or decisions that must be made.

After the press story about me having kind words about their retirements, I received a call from Deputy Chief of Staff for Communications Jocelyn Webster. She berated me for making those statements while the agency was involved in the investigation. She told me that it was "stupid" to make positive comments about them. In fact, I just thought it was honest. Once again, my communications had upset the governor's office because they felt it made the governor look bad. They would have preferred that both of them leave with a shadow of suspicion hanging over them, which I would learn was also standard operating procedure. To my knowledge, neither has ever been called to testify before any proceeding, just as I have not.

One of the biggest problems at Lincoln Hills was not with Westerhaus or Ourada, but with some of the longtime staff. They were highly averse to accepting the Trauma-Informed Care approach to juvenile corrections that had been developing over recent years. Trauma-Informed Care is backed by data on the development of youths' brains and the impact that various actions can have on them. It requires that officers engage with the youth, learn about their background, and try to understand why they act in certain ways. This was a different approach from the one that staff had been using for decades. The mindset had long been one of strict dictatorial control and physical contact. Unfortunately, change is not often a welcome word in corrections. To be honest, I wasn't sold on the idea when I arrived at the DOC, but I did take the time to get educated and eventually came to understand the value of Trauma-Informed Care, and the results were far better than what we had been getting for decades. It was all about the product that we would send back to the public, and damaging a juvenile more was not a good option.

One of the consistent themes in Trauma-Informed Care is the near elimination of things like pepper spray and prolonged lockup in segregation. The juvenile mind reacts much differently to exposure to intermediary devices for control, like pepper spray, impact weapons, or pain compliance, which can result in severe and ongoing behavioral issues. The old school of corrections tended to be more along the lines of "shut them up and lock them up," which in some cases was appropriate in the adult system. But in the juvenile system, the damage was long-lasting.

The staff who were opposed to Trauma-Informed Care did as much as they could to confound the changes the DOC needed to make. A couple of agitators encouraged staff to claim that they were feeling threatened and that the kids were out of control since Trauma-Informed Care came along. They resented not being able to "throw people in the hole," a term for segregation, or use other compliance measures they had at their disposal that resulted in instant reaction rather than evolving change. By making it into a safety issue as opposed to a difference of opinion on incarceration techniques, they would try and publicly amplify the danger they felt, claiming they were not being allowed to be tough enough on the youth. In essence, they wanted to create the image that the youth "were out of control" without the constant threat of physical or emotional deterrence looming over them.

Five days after the youth had his toes injured in the door, on December 4, 2015, DCI Administrator Dave Matthews contacted me and advised that there would be about 50 DCI agents descending on Lincoln Hills the next day to conduct interviews. They wanted the DOC to make arrangements to accommodate their investigators and have the staff held over on their shifts for interviews. Matthews had no idea what this would entail since neither he nor Paul Connell had even visited Lincoln Hills over the many months that the investigation had been going on. That alone spoke volumes about their interest in the case—an interest that suddenly shot through the roof as a youth was injured and their actions, or lack thereof, would soon be under the microscope. It was amazing to see their sudden evolution of effort that was inspired by their own exposure. The question asked by all of our staff was, "Why didn't they put this much energy into it at the beginning?" Because, if they had, much of the ensuing injuries, press coverage, expense, and turmoil would have been avoided. It would have shown the state to be proactive and decisive, rather than fumbling along as the accusations escalated.

I went to the DOJ briefing for the agents that night in Wausau before their visit to Lincoln Hills, which would ultimately be labeled by the press as a "raid." I saw many of my old DCI friends and some new agents that had come on after I left for my cabinet post. I listened as the briefing was being conducted and watched as the agents looked around somewhat perplexed as to what they were going to be doing. One agent raised his hand and asked, "Is there any evidence of a crime, like sexual assault or something else?"

The answer was, "No, there was no information like that."

Another agent raised his hand and asked, "Is there enough to even charge anyone with a crime?"

And the answer was, "Not at this time, no."

The agents started looking around at each other, and I heard one say, "What the hell are we doing here?" I wanted to blurt out that they were being used as a smokescreen by Matthews, Connell, and Schimel to try and claim that they were expending resources on a case they had botched badly. I stood silent and shared the agents' concerns.

We accommodated everything the DOJ needed, supplying interview space, feeding their agents and staff, paying overtime as we held officers past their shifts, moving inmates across the campus to interview rooms, and more. Simultaneously, I instructed our Office of Special Operations investigators to set up their own command post at Lincoln Hills to assist the DOJ in any way possible. In the grand scheme of what we had already paid in trying to effect change without DOJ's cooperation, this cost would be minimal.

It was not until after the interviews were completed and the press was in their usual feeding frenzy that we learned the DOJ had not even obtained authorization for the John Doe hearing until October 22, 2015, just six weeks before their grand "raid." This was shocking to the DOC, as we had been told by DCI Administrator Dave Matthews, who reported directly to Senior Counsel Paul Connell, that the John Doe investigation was beginning in May. For the previous six months, we had thought the John Doe investigation was ongoing. We had been given lists of employees not to speak with, which would be in line with a John Doe investigation, and the DOJ refused to share information with us under the auspices of their secret investigation. It had apparently all been a charade to get us to stop asking questions about their lack of action. From May through most of October, there had been no John Doe investigation after all.

As the situation with Lincoln Hills continued to intensify, I was being pulled between legislators and their committees demanding answers. The DOC secretary's office was contacted by Judge Mary Triggiano, head of the juvenile court system in Milwaukee County. Judge Triggiano had been involved with the DOC and our juvenile corrections operations for a long time. She had been briefed by my deputy secretary multiple times throughout the investigation and knew of the frustrations we had with the DOJ's handling of the investigation. Judge Triggiano called a meeting with the DOC, DOJ, Milwaukee County Human Services, and Milwaukee County Juvenile Detention.

I attended that meeting with my deputy secretary and assistant deputy secretary. The DOJ sent only Legal Services Administrator Dave Meaney, and there were several people there from the other Milwaukee County agencies. As we moved toward the meeting room, I saw Judge Triggiano, and she looked annoyed as we took our seats. She opened the meeting by looking right at Dave Meaney and asking, "Before we start, I want to know why in God's name this took a year to investigate?" There was a lot of uncomfortable squirming going on as Dave tried to explain that DCI had been very busy. That answer wasn't cutting it, and Dave knew it. Judge Triggiano waved off Dave's attempt to explain why the DOJ had dropped the ball and simply commented, "It's just unconscionable." The meeting went on for over an hour as each agency identified their concerns with Lincoln Hills, based largely on the reports they were reading in the paper. What made it most uncomfortable for us was that we didn't have any information we could share because the DOJ was keeping us in the dark.

When we left that meeting, I stopped Dave Meaney in the hall and said, "Dave, you need an answer for that question about why it took a year to investigate, because it is going to come up again and again." I could see the concern on his face as he understood the same thing. Unfortunately, there was no good answer they could give, and he knew it. When we left that meeting, we knew that the only thing DOJ would be able to do was shift blame.

It is difficult to imagine what it would be like to live inside a blender, but that's what it felt like. My life was consumed by a feverish press, a DOJ that was passing the buck, and a governor's office that would not let us comment on anything and left us to the wolves. The governor's deputy chief of staff of communications, Jocelyn Webster, was hell-bent on seeing our agency burn to the ground, and my DCI home agency was conducting a horrible investigation under the direction of Matthews and Connell. Add to this an attorney general who seemed to have a deer-in-the-headlights face every time Lincoln Hills was mentioned, and you had a recipe for disaster.

We had numerous staff out on paid leave pending the outcome of that investigation, and a governor who was hiding from the truth, refusing to engage at a personal level, and leaving it to his minions to create a barrier between himself and the problems. Then, of course, there was a GOP-controlled legislature that was feigning outrage after rejecting years of budget requests to fix the very problems they now faced in the press. I was sleeping about three hours a night, and my wife was worried that I was going to keel over from the stress.

Right in the middle of this churning storm, two former Walker secretaries went public about their concerns with how the governor's office insisted communications be handled. The political ground shook around the governor's office, and I didn't realize then how that would affect my future.

On December 18, 2015, an article by Dee Hall of the Wisconsin Center for Investigative Reporting appeared. It said:

Peter Bildsten, former secretary of the Department of Financial Institutions, and Paul Jadin, former head of the Wisconsin Economic Development Corp., said they were instructed in Walker's first term by then-Administration Secretary Mike Huebsch not to use official email or state telephones to relay important information or documents. Bildsten said Huebsch, Walker's top aide, gave this warning at a cabinet meeting: "Don't send me an email of anything important on my state computer, and don't call me on anything of importance on my state phone. If you have anything of consequence or importance, call me on your personal phones or walk it over."

This was a big "uh-oh" moment for many of us in the cabinet because anyone who was being honest knew it was true. The governor's communication office immediately began making damage control calls to the cabinet secretary's public information officers when the story broke, asking that they prepare statements by each secretary stating that they had never been asked to avoid creating records. When I spoke with my public information officer, she asked how I wanted to word my statement, and I told her that I couldn't make that statement because I would not lie or sacrifice my integrity.

Did I ever receive a written directive not to send emails or create records? No, of course not, that would be a record. Were my staff and

I called to the capitol countless times to deliver messages in person? Yes. Was I instructed to craft emails and letter responses that would be sent by email to intentionally create a charade of public records? Yes. Were we instructed to fax information to the governor's office to avoid creating a traceable record? Yes. Were we provided the personal cell phones of other cabinet secretaries and the governor's staff to avoid using state phones? Yes. Was I ever chastised for using state email to communicate with the high-level officials or the governor's office? Yes. Did I believe it was a ridiculous waste of taxpayer dollars to avoid public transparency? Yes.

I would learn later that other secretaries not only gave statements that they had never heard of avoiding written communications, but they started calling media outlets unsolicited, offering their ignorance of such matters or saying outright that it never happened.

The governor's office did not want to answer the question: If a public official takes overt or covert action to *avoid* creating a public record, are they evading or violating the open records law? To get the press off his back, Walker issued a directive that state agencies would answer open record requests as soon as possible. That surprised some of us considering how we had been instructed in some cases to slow down responses or not to respond to the press at all. However, with that order came the implicit understanding that underscored their longstanding position on records: Don't create any, and you won't have to worry.

The next pertinent question was, "What is a draft document, and is it a public record?" I had always been told that draft documents were not public records, and the governor's office also voiced that opinion many, many times. In fact, they had fought the release of emails concerning the "Wisconsin Idea" for a year, arguing that the documents were "drafts." In my time in state government, I never had been offered or sent to any training on the public records issues; we had lawyers that dealt with that in every agency I had worked in. Beyond that, I could understand how a draft wouldn't be a public record because it was a work in progress and subject to changes. Unless of course it served another purpose.

Meanwhile, the Lincoln Hills sausage grinder continued to churn. I was sitting at home one night not long after the DOJ raid when the phone rang. I was advised that there was supposed to be a staged uprising later that night on the female side of the institution, Copper Lake School. I advised them to have the staff there get the handheld video cameras and let the girls know they were going to record any actions. To my surprise, they told me that the video cameras didn't have any batteries that worked, and they were not sure the cameras worked either. Naturally, I told them to send someone to the store and buy some batteries. They said that nobody at the institution had a state credit card. Well, I had a state credit card. I got up and went straight to Best Buy and purchased four handheld digital video recorders with memory sticks. I then left and drove straight from my home to Lincoln Hills, arriving around 8:00 p.m. As I walked up to the front door, in my old jeans, sneakers, and a sweatshirt, the officer at the entry did a double take. "Secretary Wall! Does anyone know you're coming tonight?" I just smiled and said they would momentarily. I had been spending a lot of time at Lincoln Hills in the preceding months, but seeing me in the evening in grubby old clothes threw people for a loop. Imagine that! The secretary doesn't live in a suit and work only in the daylight. I smiled as I entered, thinking they would have loved to see pictures of me back in my narcotics days with a ponytail, beard, earring, and beat-up clothes.

I walked back to the supervisor's office, and before I could get there, the word had spread that I was on the grounds. I put the cameras on the table and told them to start opening the packages and get the batteries charged. We gave the instructions a quick glance and headed out toward the housing units. When I walked onto the floor carrying a camera, there was a sudden quiet. Most of the girls were in the common area, and all knew who I was because I had been there so much, but it was the cameras that grabbed their attention.

I went over to one of the tables where some girls were sitting, including a girl I knew to be a rather loud protagonist. I sat at the table with them, and the protagonist asked, "What are you doing up here so late?" I smiled and told her I heard there was going to be a party on the floor, and I didn't want to miss it.

She turned around with a stern look toward her fellow juveniles and turned back, obviously very perturbed, and asked, "Who told you that?"

I smiled again and said, "Someone who obviously wanted me to join the fun."

She looked at the camera on the table and asked, "What's that for?"

"To make sure that when the party starts, the right people get the credit for organizing it and attending."

She just stood up and walked away. There was no uprising that night, as I instructed the officers to keep the cameras where people could see them.

One of the officers said, "Secretary, we can't record. The batteries aren't charged."

To which I said, "They don't know that." I gave the officer a smile and a wink as I headed out. The situation was in hand; crisis averted.

Many people heard about my late-night shopping and travel to meet with the girls, both at the institution and at DOC headquarters. I was asked several times why I didn't just delegate someone else to buy the batteries, go to the institution, and meet at the housing unit. And my answer was simple: "If people don't see my commitment to fixing things, no matter when it is needed, and how inconvenient it may be, how can I expect them to share that commitment?" Lead by example, not decree.

It was a few days later that the yearly cabinet Christmas party was held at the executive residence. By this time, my wife, Debi, was pretty disgusted with all that was happening and the efforts by Walker and Schimel to dodge responsibility. She told me that she wasn't going to attend the party as she had in years past because she was afraid she would tell Walker off. Deputy Secretary Dede Morgan and I got there early because I was going to stay only a short time and head back to Lincoln Hills that night. Although it was the season of celebration, my mind could not escape the quagmire at Lincoln Hills.

When we walked in, the governor and Lieutenant Governor Becky Kleefisch were standing in the foyer talking. Becky turned to see us and immediately said, "Oh my God, come here, you two!" and she walked toward us with her arms outstretched. She gave us both a hug and encouraged us to stay strong.

I then turned to the governor, and he shook my hand, asking, "How are you holding up?" I was honest in telling him that it was a challenge. We talked very openly about how the DOJ had dragged its feet on the investigation at Lincoln Hills, and he agreed. I related the comments made by Judge Triggiano at the Milwaukee meeting and how she had captured the frustration in one question: "Why in God's name did this take a year to investigate?" He agreed with her and lamented that things did not have to go this way and sympathized with us that we were left trying to fix problems in an information vacuum. He expressed a few times that he knew we were doing everything we could and thanked us for staying strong.

He then asked if things were starting to calm down, which surprised and concerned me considering the press coverage. I told him that they were not calming down, and in fact, it seemed like the DOJ was gearing up to try and get the entire case out of their lap and toss it to the U.S. Attorney's Office. My guess was they would use the pretext that "something very big is going on here and needs federal review," even though not a single person had been charged with a crime. I told the governor that I was concerned that this would be shifting the spotlight back on the DOC, and on him, with the veiled implication that something very bad was happening, while maintaining they could not comment because the federal authorities were involved. He just nodded, as if he understood, but didn't comment.

I apologized to the governor that I would not be staying long at the party because I was heading back north to Lincoln Hills. He thanked me again for the hard work we were doing and told me that he fully supported us. He said, "I'm sorry for all of the mud you are being dragged through." And then he put his hand on my shoulder, adding, "I've been there and know how hard it can be."

I just looked at him thinking, "You have no idea." The mud I was being dragged through could be affected with leadership on his part. The Mud he was dragged through was a result of his own actions.

On my drive north to Lincoln Hills, after having spoken with the governor for the longest period of time since the drama began, I had a thought creep into my mind that caused me to shiver. Could the governor and the attorney general be working together to sweep Lincoln Hills under the rug and put the blame on me and the agency? That would explain the DOJ's foot-dragging and the apparent lack of interest on the part of the governor's chief of staff, Rich Zipperer. The governor's office was constantly updated on our concerns about the lack of progress with the DOJ investigation but never did anything about it. Schimel had likewise been kept up to date but always acted like he didn't know what was going on. Maybe Walker and Schimel were setting up an exit plan through a federal agency referral, which could take years to complete. And what would bring the story to a neat little wrap-up before the handoff to the feds? Change the leadership of the DOC and move along with vague assurances the problems had been addressed and a new DOC savior would be brought in.

Sure enough, the DOJ advised the DOC just days later that they were going to be referring the Lincoln Hills investigation over to the U.S. Attorney's Office "for review." My guess was that Paul Connell, who was a former assistant U.S. attorney, had spoken to his friend and former coworker John Vaudreuil, the U.S. attorney in the Western District of Wisconsin, and asked him to "take" the case. Connell understood that sending the case into the federal system with such a broad purview could bury the case for years, or at least past the next election, still over two years away. The legitimate question asked many times was, "If the attorney general investigated this case for a year and could not find a single charge to bring against anyone, then what does he think referring it to the federal government will do?" The answer to that question, lingering now for over three years, remains unanswered.

In an article in the *Milwaukee Journal Sentinel* in December 2016, the attorney general demonstrated the commitment to the case his office had exhibited all along. Schimel claimed he was in the dark as to what the federal government had been doing with the case for the last year since he ditched it. He also stated, "It wasn't immediately looking like it was as pervasive as it seems now to have been." When the attorney general of Wisconsin said that he didn't immediately know how bad the problem was with Lincoln Hills, then he simply did not tell the truth, because I had told him personally several times and his people investigated it for over a year. Blame shifting 101: "If only I had known ..."

After Schimel's "in the dark" comment was published, along with the fact that the FBI hadn't been up to Lincoln Hills for nearly a year, Schimel changed course and announced that he was "considering" reopening his department's probe and that he "might" issue charges over alleged inmate abuses. However, it would appear that Schimel never did reopen his investigation, and it seemed this claim was just another attempt to divert the press and buy time for the public to hopefully forget what the DOJ and the governor had *not* done.

Legislators from both parties took the time to travel to Lincoln Hills to see the institution and conditions themselves. I went with many of them to be available to answer questions and engage in discussions. However, the fact that Walker refused to even step foot into the institution, even to this day, spoke volumes to me, my executive staff, and just about everyone watching the circus that had developed.

Walker brought me in to run Corrections but forgot to mention that he would not support any changes beyond words. He had a fundamental misunderstanding of the challenges of the agency and would not commit funding to address those challenges in any meaningful way. Why? Because it was against his ingrained vision of crime and punishment, a vision he had enacted into legislation

20 years before. It was also against his "no taxes" political tag line that he worked so hard to maintain. It was ironic that a cop who was responsible for putting many people in prison over the years could evolve on this issue, while a governor who never set foot inside the prison or arrested a single person could not. Maybe it was because felons could not vote.

It is worth noting that despite what Brad Schimel and the DOJ alluded to in stating they felt I would be called to testify on the Lincoln Hills issues before some unknown federal entity, I have never been called to testify or even been interviewed about the case by any entity whatsoever, including Schimel's DOJ. Why was I never called to testify during the DOJ's investigation or in any federal proceeding? Because the DOJ and the governor's office know what I would have talked about, and it wouldn't benefit them. ♦

FORCED OUT

On Friday, January 29, 2015, I was on my way to Lincoln Hills to spend another weekend walking the housing units to talk with staff and youth as I had done many days over the previous four months, just trying to ease the stress. My phone rang, and the caller ID showed it was Rich Zipperer. Anyone who works at the upper levels of state government knows that bad news is usually handled at the end of the day on Friday. This was to be no different. Zipperer asked me to meet him in his office at 5:00 p.m. I turned around and headed back to Madison. I was pretty confident that this would be the end of my time at DOC, but to be honest, it was almost a relief. By this time, it all just felt so dirty.

I arrived at the governor's office and went into Zipperer's office, where Department of Administration Secretary Scott Neitzel was also waiting. Rich opened the conversation by saying, "You are coming in tonight as the DOC secretary, and you will be leaving here as the DOC secretary," in an effort to relieve my stress. I told him that was nice, but I was sure that was not why he had called me to the capitol.

Rich said that he and Neitzel had been talking, and they thought that maybe we should start planning for a transition at the DOC in the next few months. My prediction of the chain of events was falling into place. I asked him if that "transition" would involve me leaving my position, and he just shrugged. I was a bit irate that they were choosing to do this while the investigation was going on and expressed my concern that the press would play it as "Secretary Ed Wall resigns amid Lincoln Hills scandal." Rich explained that was why they wanted to do something down the road a bit to give the press a chance to calm down. I told Rich, as I had told him and his deputy chief of staff, Matt Moroney, dozens of times, this was not going to calm down until the governor and the legislature decided to do something rather than ignore the problem. I couldn't help but think back to Zipperer's comment about the governor and legislature needing to be sued in order to get something done.

My wife and kids had spoken to me for months about leaving the DOC because they were worried about what it was doing to me. That past summer I had made some inquiries quietly to DOA about returning to the DCI but held off because I wanted to get Lincoln Hills resolved. The DOJ had told us at that time that everything was wrapped up, and we looked forward to finally moving forward. Believing the DOJ was a mistake, as the next several months showed.

On the night of my conversation with Rich and Scott, the DCI deputy administrator position was vacant, and a recruitment process was in progress to fill it. I knew that if I resigned, I could return to my DCI administrator position, as guaranteed by law and state policy, and Dave Matthews could drop back into the open deputy administrator position. This thought had crossed my mind already when I saw the position was open, and I would be only too happy to return to my law enforcement career.

I told Rich that I was going to make this easy on him and advised him about the DCI deputy administrator position being open and that I wanted to resign and return to the DOJ. That was not what they were expecting. Rich stammered, looked around nervously, and repeated that they wanted to wait a few months to make the move. I told him that I understood what *they* wanted to do, but my concern for what *they* wanted was not the first thing on my mind at that point. They had unsheathed their knives, so it was my move. I did not want the DCI to fill the deputy administrator position and then have to demote or lay off someone who would be bumped upon my lawful restoration.

Then the truth for their desired delay came out. Rich explained that they didn't want me to leave anytime soon because they didn't want to have to deal with putting a new secretary through confirmation hearings. They were trying to delay the announcement so the Senate would be out of session until the following fall. Rich went on to explain that if they had to go through confirmation hearings, it would become a circus sideshow with the Democrats attacking the governor over Lincoln Hills. As you can imagine, this did not move me to tears. In fact, I thought that maybe it would force them to finally do something. Nothing moved this administration on corrections issues, but maybe the legislature would if there was enough pressure ... or a lawsuit.

Ultimately, I agreed to submit my resignation with an effective date in March, after the Senate was scheduled to go out, if Rich would contact the DOJ and ask them to stop the recruitment for the deputy administrator position pending my restoration. He told me he would contact the DOJ and speak with them. I left the governor's office with a head-spinning mix of emotions. In one respect, I was disappointed that the governor had decided it was time to sacrifice me to change the story, but you come into those positions knowing that you are expendable. On the other hand, I was excited to get back to the DCI and the position I loved and probably never should have left. I was going home, or so I thought.

I would learn the next day from a friend at the capitol that shortly after I left the governor's office, former DOC Secretary Jon Litscher, who served under Tommy Thompson, went in to meet with Zipperer and Neitzel. They obviously had a plan, which was fine with me. Whether their plan and mine would coincide would remain to be seen.

As a harbinger of things to come, when Connell and Cook first found out that I intended to restore to my position with the DCI, they sent Schimel an email advising him. Schimel's ominous response was, "This will get interesting," which clearly showed that he had no intention of me ever returning to my position, despite the law and state policy.

That weekend was an emotional roller coaster as I went home to wrestle with my conscience. I was truly looking forward to returning to my law enforcement career and the DCI. On the other hand, I felt as if I was abandoning the DOC at the height of the storm that had developed around Lincoln Hills. However, that decision was not mine, and I was resigned to the fact that the governor and the GOP-controlled legislature simply did not want to fix the problems. As with most things at that level, it is management by crisis rather than management by reason and prudence. The problems at the DOC would not be fixed absent the governor and legislature's commitment to a growing problem that had been created over decades. Despite all the proposals we had made to them over the preceding three years, they were intent on taking no action until forced to.

As I took stock over the weekend of all that had happened and all that was about to happen, I was faced with another sickening thought. By returning to the DCI, I would be working for Attorney General Brad Schimel and Senior Counsel Paul Connell, two men that I absolutely did not respect or trust. If your intentions are honorable and you lead with your heart and your actions speak to your honest intent, I will follow you through the gates of hell. Neither Schimel nor Connell inspired or earned anything close to that type of loyalty or devotion. I just hoped I could keep the DCI above the political fray, but I was not optimistic.

Throughout the Lincoln Hills issues, Connell made it his practice to surprise us with conference calls that we were not expecting, always with others on the phone. It was as if Connell wanted witnesses on the calls but didn't want you to have the same advantage. He always seemed insecure to me, even as an assistant U.S. attorney, and he took refuge in having others with him when he would contact us. My legal staff expressed their dismay with his tactics on multiple occasions. I would read later in an article involving the Department of Public Instruction Superintendent, Tony Evers, that he had experienced the same thing in dealing with the DOJ. This was a new tactic that flowed into the DOJ with Schimel and Connell. It had the effect of immediately putting the other parties on the call in a defensive mode whenever the DOJ called. It got to the point where my staff wouldn't want to speak with the DOJ by phone because they always had the feeling the DOJ staff were setting them up for an ambush.

On February 4, 2016, I received an email from Connell, which on the surface appeared friendly and cordial, as Connell usually did. Unfortunately, I had learned already through experience that Connell was a slippery ambush artist, so I was immediately on guard. He said in the note he would like me to be available that afternoon for a quick call with him and Deputy Attorney General Andy Cook to "catch up," which I had hoped would be to discuss the logistics of my return to the DCI but knew it wouldn't be. To test my theory, I replied that I was going to be at the capitol later that day for meetings and offered to stop by the office since it was across the street. He replied back tersely, "We will agree to a phone call. What time will you be available?" Bingo. Leopards don't change their spots.

It didn't take long for Connell to drop the facade of cordiality. He was too much of a coward to meet in person and did not want to have to look someone in the face when he intended to deliver bad news. I was not surprised by this at all, as my cop instinct had told me what Connell was like a long time ago. It is far easier to try and intimidate people over a phone call or email than it is to sit and talk with them. Connell preferred to deal from a venue where he couldn't be seen.

We subsequently had that call on the afternoon of February 4, 2016, and I asked my deputy secretary and legal chief to join me on the call from my office because I could not trust Connell as far as I could throw a piano. When we called in for the supposed call between Connell, Cook, and me to "catch up," Connell announced that there were seven other attorneys in the room with him. I just shook my head as he announced the cadre of legal wizards he had at his side to hold him up. He was true to form once again.

Connell was painfully aware that I had been questioning the DOJ's response to Lincoln Hills for months. He knew that I had raised the issue multiple times with the governor, the governor's subordinates, the attorney general, and the DOJ itself. His disgust with me for raising that awareness was apparent. It could have caused the attorney general to question Connell's leadership ability, though for some reason it did not. According to Zipperer, Connell had supposedly been contacted by the governor's office on multiple occasions regarding my and the governor's concerns with the length of time the investigation was taking and the lack of resource commitment by the attorney general. Connell had also been the one that coordinated the obfuscation of the DOJ's inept response to Lincoln Hills and the skyrocketing costs the DOC was absorbing because of the slow-motion handling of the issues. Connell had much to worry about.

After announcing the other attorneys in the room, Connell stated that he was conveying the "intent of the attorney general" in how my restoration to my former position as DCI administrator would be handled. He then advised me that the DOJ would be placing me immediately on administrative leave with pay because they were investigating issues involving the agency I was running as a cabinet secretary. Connell said that the DOJ felt there was a conflict of interest in me returning to the DCI in light of the ongoing Lincoln Hills investigation. He then advised me that I would be reinstated to my DCI administrator position *for one day*, and then I would be transferred to a non-law enforcement position in a different division. They were obviously trying to end my career and push me out of the DOJ.

Immediately, I advised Connell and his bevy of attorneys that what they were doing was in violation of state laws, DOA policies, and a clear abuse of authority. Connell responded, "You do realize the attorney general can appoint anyone he wants to the DCI administrator position, don't you?" Of course, I disagreed because that position was a protected civil service position and not an unclassified appointment that the attorney general could appoint or remove at will. I then advised him that the state laws on restoration from the unclassified service under Wisconsin State Statute 230.33 and DOA memo MRS-211 were applicable. Connell responded that it was their opinion that they could make these changes. I told him that I would be forced to appeal their decision.

Connell then stated that since I would be appealing the decision, that all future communications with the DOJ should be in writing only. This would ensure that he wouldn't have to ever face me or have an intelligent conversation about the future. It also ensured that I wouldn't have a chance to speak with Schimel, who also wanted to hide behind legal barricades. These were not men of honor; they were cowards. Another painful lesson was learned that day: Never tell a bunch of attorneys that they are violating the law because they will expend every effort to twist that law to their point of view as directed by their boss.

I hung up from that call and immediately called Rich Zipperer. I told Rich what had transpired on the call and that what the DOJ was doing was illegal, violated state policy, and was an abuse of authority by the attorney general. I asked Rich if he had known what the DOJ was planning to do to me, and he said he was not aware. I then asked him if he was familiar with the laws of restoration or the state policies regarding restoration, and he said he was not. Rich was obviously uncomfortable and said something along the lines of, "This is an employment issue between you and the DOJ." I explained to Rich that this was far more than an employment issue between me and the DOJ; this was about the laws of restoration and political appointees. I also explained the chilling effect this could have in the future if the restoration laws were going to be so flagrantly manipulated by politicians in their own interests.

Shortly after I spoke with Rich, I spoke with the governor by phone and explained to him what the DOJ was planning to do to me in trying to restore my position. I asked the governor if he had known the DOJ was going to do this to me, and he said he had not. I then asked him if he was familiar with the laws of restoration, and he stated he was not. I explained that the law and state policy guaranteed civil servants who leave their positions to serve in gubernatorial positions the right to return to their former positions, and he seemed to understand. I also reminded him that I was guaranteed restoration to my position by his staff, DOJ staff, state law, and state policy prior to accepting the appointment. He said that he understood.

In one of our subsequent calls, Walker expressed his concern for what Schimel was trying to do to me. The governor knew how much my law enforcement career meant to me because we had discussed it many times. He also knew that I would have never accepted his cabinet appointment if it meant I would be forced out of my career, because I had rejected their first offer to head the DOC for that reason. He told me that he would reach out to Schimel personally and added, "It's time for Brad to step in here and make the right decisions and stop letting his staff make them for him. This is just wrong." When I hung up, I felt that Walker understood that the DOJ was violating the law and state policies, and he could make it right. My last hope was a false hope. Scott Walker would do what he always does and slip quietly behind a press spokesperson with prepared comments.

Zipperer called me to his office the next day and asked, "Is there another job you would want outside of the DOJ? They don't want you back." My gut wrenched as I heard those words. It wasn't that the DOJ didn't want me back. The DCI was my home agency, the agency I had applied to three times when I lived in New Hampshire, the agency I traveled across the country for with my family, the agency that I had toiled for, day and night, for 16 years. I remember thinking to myself, "How would Schimel take it if I was his boss and just decided that he should work in a job shuffling paper clips, rather than the job he trained for, received certification to perform in, and had presumably dedicated his life to?" Not well, I'm sure. Schimel was not a career state agency employee; he was a career politician and a limited-term employee.

I explained to Zipperer that the DOJ had no choice, and by law, they had to give me my job back. My DCI administrator job was a civil service position that I competed for and not an appointed position where I served at the attorney general's pleasure. I also explained that my career was in law enforcement, my certification was in law enforcement, and my retirement was in the protective category by virtue of my position as a sworn law enforcement officer. By forcibly demoting me into a non-law enforcement position, the DOJ would be harming my retirement and my family. After explaining all the negative things that the DOJ intended to do to me, I had hoped that Zipperer would begin to grasp the severity of what was happening. Instead, he stared at me like a dead fish. He then said, "Well, there must be some other job you would want?" I wanted to stick a pipe cleaner in his ear to see if it would come out the other side.

I explained to Zipperer there were no other jobs in state government comparable to the DCI administrator. He then said, "You are lucky you have the right to a job. Why won't you take something else? I don't have any right to a job. People understand these things can happen when they take governor appointments."

Therein lay the problem. I had a politician who accepted a political appointment from another politician with no restoration rights trying to twist my situation into his own. Across the street, two other politicians also saw no reason to abide by the laws and policies put in place to safeguard against this level of arrogance, abuse of authority, violation of law, and lack of concern for civil servants. I was stuck between arrogance and ignorance.

"Rich, you don't get it," I told him. "I turned down the request to lead the DOC initially because I was on probation as DCI administrator and nothing meant more in my professional life than that position. Then I was approached again for the position, and I was told that I was needed. I was *promised* by the governor's office, the

DOJ, the law, and state policy that I would get my job back at the end of my service in the DOC, and now that is being thrown out the window." Even after trying to explain to him that the DOJ was effectively demoting me, destroying my career, and causing harm to my family without so much as just cause or due process, he still looked like a trout lying on an ice blanket in the grocery store.

When it was clear I could not get through Rich's mental block, I told him that I would file an appeal and may end up having to file lawsuits to right the wrongs that he was about to let happen. He shrugged it off. I went back to my office and drew up my letter of resignation. I submitted it to the governor's office that day, and the cat would be out of the bag, Senate confirmations be damned.

My letter of resignation to the governor was polite and professional.

February 5, 2016

Governor Scott Walker
Wisconsin State Capitol

Dear Governor Walker,

For over three years I have had the honor and privilege to lead your largest cabinet agency, the Wisconsin Department of Corrections. Throughout my tenure, we have focused on modernizing practices, creating fair policies, developing leadership, reforming segregation, improving mental health care and responding to the ever-changing philosophy of corrections reform. Our management team is proud of the many accomplishments we have made and know that the Department is a better place because of them.

The vast majority of the men and women of the Department of Corrections are committed professionals who perform their duties in spite of the many challenges they face. With over 10,000 employees in 4 divisions, 38 institutions, 10 regional offices, 120 field offices and 90,000 people in some form of incarceration, probation or parole, the potential for unforeseen and dangerous interactions is a constant reality that they deal with every single day.

The work of corrections often draws emotion and conjecture from many due to the nature of the responsibilities the Department is tasked with. However, regardless of where those feelings may fall, staff at the Department of Corrections deserves the support, gratitude and respect of the administration, the legislature and the citizens of Wisconsin.

After considerable thought, reflection and consultation with my family, I believe that the time has come to turn the page for the Department of Corrections and step aside to allow a new person with fresh perspectives to lead the agency forward. Please accept this letter of resignation from my cabinet position to be effective on March 19th, 2016. I will work with the administration in the coming weeks to facilitate a smooth transition for the new leadership you will appoint. Thank you for the opportunity to have served the state in this critically important public safety role.

Most Sincerely,
Edward F. Wall

SABOTAGING MY CAREER

F ive days later, I submitted my letter of restoration to Schimel with attachments. The letter went into detail about the laws of restoration and how I looked forward to rejoining my DOJ family. It also acknowledged that the Lincoln Hills investigation, which I had personally requested, was ongoing and I asked that "investigative firewalls" be put in place to assure that the integrity of the investigation could not be questioned. With the letter, I also sent along documents that included state policy MRS-211 and state laws dealing with restoration.

In a personal letter that I included in a sealed envelope for Schimel, I bared my soul and expressed my concerns over the way I had been treated so far in what I had hoped would be a homecoming, but instead was turning into a nightmare. It had no impact on Schimel. In fact, I had tried to call Schimel, sent him text messages and emails wishing to meet with him, and he never acknowledged one of them. Pretty strange way to treat a returning administrator and executive staff member in his agency, or so I thought.

Seeing as the DOJ had already proclaimed that they had handed the Lincoln Hills investigation over to the feds, there should have been no reason to block my return. However, they would go to extremes to try and explain why I could not return in the days ahead.

The press got word of my resignation a few days later, and as predicted, the headline was that I was resigning amid the probe. The headline and veiled comments by the attorney general were designed to cast some kind of sinister light on me, but the fact was the governor just wanted to find a reason to change the story. The term "falling on your sword" was not invented that day, but it didn't make the sword hurt any less. I became physically ill and went into the bathroom in my office and vomited. I was having my first ever, but unfortunately not the last, panic attack of my life. I was in a cold sweat, my fingers tingled, and my nausea would not subside.

My reputation was being forever tarnished by politicians who could not muster the courage to face the challenges themselves. It was character assassination sanctioned by the governor and carried out by his attorney general.

One week after I submitted my resignation letter and while I was still at the DOC, I looked at the news and saw that Governor Walker had, in fact, been notified by a Racine County judge of problems at Lincoln Hills in February of 2012—four years earlier, and 10 months before I was appointed secretary! I was stunned and angry. When I first briefed the governor's office in November 2014 on the Lincoln Hills issues, there was not a whisper that they had heard about problems there before. I was confident that Walker must have gotten the message because it came from a judge. That is not the type of letter that would be relegated to an office lackey to respond to, at least not without advising Walker himself since it could be a landmine issue.

When I saw the letter printed in the paper, I saw that it had "Alex I /Policy" handwritten on it. I knew that meant the letter was reviewed by Alex Ignatowski, one of the governor's closer aides, who was working in the policy area. Alex was also the husband of Katie Ignatowski, one of the governor's attorneys who would become his legal chief.

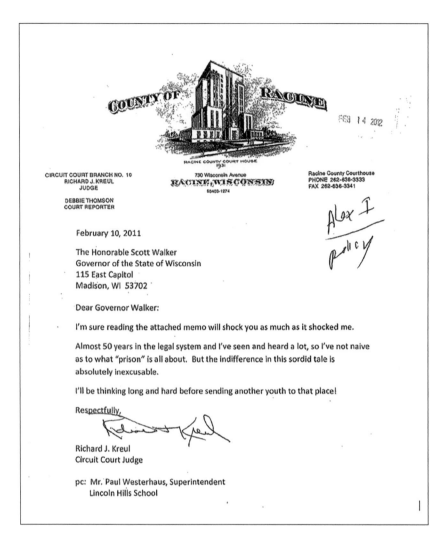

CIRCUIT COURT BRANCH NO. 10
RICHARD J. KREUL
JUDGE

DEBBIE THOMSON
COURT REPORTER

730 Wisconsin Avenue
RACINE, WISCONSIN
53403-1274

Racine County Courthouse
PHONE 262-636-3333
FAX 262-636-3341

RACINE COUNTY COURT HOUSE
1931

COUNTY OF RACINE

FEB 14 2012

Alex I
policy

February 10, 2011

The Honorable Scott Walker
Governor of the State of Wisconsin
115 East Capitol
Madison, WI 53702

Dear Governor Walker:

I'm sure reading the attached memo will shock you as much as it shocked me.

Almost 50 years in the legal system and I've seen and heard a lot, so I've not naive as to what "prison" is all about. But the indifference in this sordid tale is absolutely inexcusable.

I'll be thinking long and hard before sending another youth to that place!

Respectfully,

Richard J. Kreul
Circuit Court Judge

pc: Mr. Paul Westerhaus, Superintendent
Lincoln Hills School

The idea that Alex, with his political and policy experience, would have reviewed that judge's letter with the explosive information it contained and not discussed it with the governor was not in the realm of possibility. But it was in the well-known realm of deniability.

Since the governor's office was aware of the accusations raised by the judge four years before, I couldn't help but wonder if he and Schimel agreed to try and keep everything involving Lincoln Hills quiet. Political aspirations and goals had impacted the decisions made in many of Walker and Schimel's actions. Could this be no different? In my mind, it was not beyond the scope of what these two would do to protect their positions and political futures.

On February 15, 2016, I received two letters from the DOJ. The first was from the DOJ director of Human Resources advising me that I was being restored to my position as the DCI administrator effective February 28, 2016, what my pay rate was, and that Connell would be my direct supervisor.

February 15, 2016

Edward F. Wall, Jr.
6672 Highland Dr.
Windsor WI 53598

Dear Mr. Wall:

This letter acknowledges and confirms your request to be restored to the Administrator, Division of Criminal Investigation position in the Department of Justice. Your assigned headquarters will be the Risser Justice Building, located at 17 W. Main St., Madison, WI. This appointment is a Career Executive position in pay schedule 81-01 and is effective February 28, 2016. Your supervisor will be Senior Counsel Paul Connell.

In accordance with the pay on appointment provisions contained in the 2015-2017 State of Wisconsin Compensation Plan, upon your appointment, your salary will be $51.96 per hour or $108,076 annually.

The work you will be performing is exempt from the overtime provisions of the Fair Labor Standards Act (FLSA), which means that you are a salaried employee and, therefore, not eligible for payment of overtime under this law. You may be required to account for your work absences by either working additional time or by using your paid leave.

Sincerely,
Jayne Swingen
Human Resources Director

The second letter advised me that I was being placed on administrative leave immediately pending the outcome of the Lincoln Hills investigation that I had requested.

February 15, 2016

Edward F. Wall, Jr.
6672 Highland Drive
Windsor, WI 53598

Dear Mr. Wall,

Effective February 27, 2016 you will be placed on paid administrative leave from your Department of Justice (DOJ) Division of Criminal Investigation (DCI) Administrator position pending conclusion of the investigation into Lincoln Hills School for Boys and Copper Lake School for Girls. Since you were responsible for both institutions while you were Department of Corrections Secretary and requested the investigation, DOJ is placing you on paid administrative leave given the clear conflict of interest.

During your paid administrative leave, you are not to perform any duties as DCI Administrator, nor are you to report to any DOJ site or act on behalf of the DOJ. As a result, your DOJ identification and security access cards will not be provided to you and you are not to use any security access card in your possession to enter any DOJ facility. While your DOJ email account will be active, you may only use that account for the purpose of communicating with me or Senior Counsel Paul W. Connell. You are not to make any affirmative work—related contact with any other DOJ employee.

Andrew C. Cook
Deputy Attorney General

The restoration letter was shocking, and the restrictions laid out were outright punitive in nature. But there was a reason for the restrictions they placed on me, and that reason was they did not want me to see how the Lincoln Hills investigation had been handled, even though we had figured that out months before. It didn't take a rocket scientist to listen to their briefing in my conference room at the DOC to know they had much to conceal. They also made it clear that they had no intention of ever letting me back into the DOJ, regardless of what they said in the letter from Cook. What other reason could there be in refusing to even give me my state employee ID card, which all state employees were required to have? I knew then that this was a setup, and they intended to drive me out of my career. In that letter, it clearly stated that I was being placed on leave from my DCI administrator position pending the conclusion of the investigation into Lincoln Hills School for Boys and Copper Lake School for Girls. That was a lie before they wrote it, as they already told me on the conference call that they were ending my law enforcement career one day after I would restore. But it made them look like they were following the restoration laws. It was a farce that they would release to the press.

My restoration to the DCI was effective on February 28, 2016, and the next day, as they told me they would, I received two more letters from the DOJ.

March 1, 2016

Edward F. Wall, Jr.
6672 Highland Dr.
Windsor, WI 53598

Dear Mr. Wall,

This letter confirms your career executive reassignment to the Program and Policy Manager (Deputy Division Administrator) position in the Department of Justice, Division of Law Enforcement Services. This appointment will be effective March 20, 2016, and your supervisor will be Senior Counsel Paul Connell.

This career executive reassignment is a permanent civil service movement under the authority of ER-MRS 30.07, Wisconsin Administrative Code. Your salary will remain $51.96 per hour.

Andrew Cook
Deputy Attorney General

....

March 1, 2016

Edward F. Wall, Jr.
6672 Highland Dr.
Windsor, WI 53598

Dear Mr. Wall,

This letter confirms that your current paid administrative leave from the Department of Justice (DOJ), which began on February 28, 2016, will remain in effect with your March 20, 2016 career executive reassignment to the Division of Law Enforcement Services Program and Policy Manager position until further notice.

During your paid administrative leave, you are not to perform any DOJ duties, nor are you to report to any DOJ site or act on behalf of DOJ. You are not to make any affirmative work-related contact with any other DOJ employee. You may use your DOJ e-mail account only for the purpose of communications with me or Senior Counsel Paul W. Connell.

Andrew Cook
Deputy Attorney General

The letters advised me that I was being transferred to a program and policy manager position in the Division of Law Enforcement Services. It was a civilian position and not in my "protective status" retirement that I had built my career on. The forced transfer and demotion gave no reason for the actions, as was required under state regulation ER-MRS 30.07(2), which states, "All such reassignments shall be made in writing to the affected employee, **with the reasons stated therein.**" Schimel, Wisconsin's top cop, was ending a real cop's career for no reason other than his own agenda.

During the preceding weeks, I had spoken to the governor on a few different occasions concerning what the DOJ was doing to me. I begged him to step in and stop the attorney general from breaking the law, violating state restoration policy, and crucifying a cabinet secretary who had served him faithfully. These were requests I should have never had to make. I explained that the spectacle of this playing out in the courts was unnecessary and he could stop it. He told me that he would make arrangements to meet with Schimel and get this straightened out.

Subsequently, I received a call from Zipperer, stating that the governor was going to meet with Schimel the following week to discuss my restoration issues. I asked him if I should be there, and he said that he would rather not have me there so they could have a frank discussion. I was scheduled to go to Florida that following week with my family to try and decompress for a few days after the unending nightmare they had been putting us through.

I told Zipperer that I had the first draft of my transfer appeal for the Wisconsin Employment Relations Commission (WERC), and I would bring a copy to him at the capitol to brief the governor with. The draft outlined the laws, state policies, and circumstances surrounding my lawful restoration. Zipperer quickly backpedaled and said he did not want me to bring it to the capitol because he didn't want a copy "laying around" the office. It was the same reason they often used for not wanting the DOC to leave them with any records that could make them officially aware of issues. After I explained that the information would be useful for his briefing to the governor before meeting with Schimel, Zipperer said, "Wouldn't that look great, you briefing me on the law?" You see, Zipperer was also a lawyer, and he felt that a neophyte like myself telling him how to brief the governor on legal issues wouldn't look good. Personally, I didn't care how it looked.

My frustration with the administration's aversion to creating, holding, or even acknowledging records was now boiling over since Zipperer was using their "no records" mantra to try and shield himself and the governor from being adequately informed about my dilemma. I knew that they would claim later that the governor and his staff were not aware of any issues concerning my restoration. That was the same line they used when the Racine judge's letter concerning Lincoln Hills became public. It was all about deniability. And all the while, the governor would tell the press that he wished me well in my return to my law enforcement career.

My mind was in a state of turmoil as the reality of abandonment loomed above me. How could this man, a governor whom I reluctantly agreed to serve, not step in to ensure the law was followed and his promises kept? It was because I didn't matter anymore. They were changing the story, and my view from under the bus wasn't going to change anything. I called Zipperer's cell phone and left him a message asking for his home email address so I could send him the draft to review since he and the governor were mentioned in it. Zipperer called me back the next day, and we spoke. He said that he didn't want me sending the draft document to his personal email because he didn't want to have a record. I told him then that it was simply a draft document, and my understanding was that it was not a record. I just wanted him and the governor to be adequately informed before speaking with Schimel. Zipperer said that he was well enough informed to brief the governor.

When I hung up the phone, it occurred to me that the people who were already briefing Zipperer were likely Paul Connell and Deputy Attorney General Andy Cook—the very same people who were keeping me out of my job and twisting the laws to their liking. That was why Zipperer didn't want me there for the meeting, because it was likely going to be a strategy session on how to make me disappear. At that moment, I decided I was going to mail the draft to Zipperer's house so I could at least be sure he received it. If I mailed it to the office, they would do the same thing they did with the judge's letter and claim it never got to Zipperer or the governor. With that draft, I included a note that said:

Hi Rich,

I know that you didn't want me sending this electronically or to the office because of the records issue, so I elected instead to send it to your home in writing and would ask that you feel free to shred it once you've looked it over. Nobody will know that I sent it and this is strictly between you and me. I understand the concern the administration has over creating records Rich, but I can't let that harm me or my family worse than we've already been harmed.

As an attorney, I'm guessing that you would want to know how strong your position is before you advocate for me or the boss. If you don't, then you won't be prepared to press forward on solid ground. As the governor said to me the other day, "It's time for Brad to step in here and make the right decisions and stop letting his staff make them for him. This is just wrong." What I'm seeking is nothing more than what the law guaranteed me when I took the DOC job.

You and I both know that this is strictly a personal issue between Matthews and Connell in trying to keep Matthews in place. I also know they have been talking to JB, who tried this same stunt with Jim Warren when he was administrator and Jim just elected to retire. JB is still pissed at me because I didn't promote his wife into the chief legal position and went to Eric in an attempt to override me. That's where his great advice stems from and I would rather not dredge that all up. They are trying to push me the same way and I know that Connell made the comment "He'll probably just leave and go get a police chief job somewhere." I won't be doing that and have at least 10 more years to work.

My proposed solution is at the end of the document, but you should read it all since you and the boss are both mentioned in it. I kept those references to a minimum intentionally. I absolutely do not want to file a lawsuit or engage attorneys in any way Rich, I just want to go back to the job I should have never left. But if I'm forced to advocate for myself, it will be with the usual effort I put into everything. Thanks Rich and I appreciate anything you can do to fix this mess.

Ed

That letter, driven by sheer desperation created by Walker, Zipperer, Connell, and Schimel, was the biggest mistake of my life. Though it was nothing more than a last-ditch attempt by a faithful public servant who had devoted over three decades of his life to public safety to save his career, Zipperer and the DOJ seized on it as a reason to get rid of me under the pretext that I was advocating for the destruction of a public record. They knew that was not the case, but that would be the story they would put out.

Two days after I mailed the letter, I received a letter by email and later by U.S. mail from Zipperer.

March 11, 2016

Secretary Wall:

Yesterday, March 10, 2016, I received at my home address a letter from you via U.S. Mail regarding your employment situation after leaving the Department of Corrections. The letter enclosed a document titled "Wisconsin Employment Relations Commission Career Executive Reassignment Appeal."

After reading your cover letter, I want to make it clear that the letter is not an accurate representation of our conversations regarding the manner in which we handle records in our administration. In this situation, you requested my personal email address, which I declined to provide, because the record you proposed to send to me related to official business. In addition, there was no need to send our office a draft pleading relating to an employment issue between you and the Wisconsin Department of Justice.

As a former member of our administration, you understand that we are expected to fully and dutifully follow all public records laws and procedures. I have a duty to retain your correspondence as an official record and it will be treated as such.

While I have not yet had time to review each of the statements and claims in the entire correspondence, I felt it imperative to relay to you, as soon as possible, my concerns with some of the suggestions included in your letter.

Since this is a Wisconsin Department of Justice personnel matter, the appropriate place to send official communications regarding your employment is to the DOJ.

Sincerely,
Rich Zipperer

It wasn't lost on me that Zipperer elected to respond to me in an official letter and sent it by email. He was loading his own cannon and would use his response against me in creating a record that they could release, just as he had done with a letter previously on Lincoln Hills. He could have just picked up the phone and called, but he did not. He did not want to use the same method of communication that the administration had insisted on during my entire time at the DOC. Instead, they would move to cut my throat with the very open records issue they had avoided for so long. I'm sure Schimel's office saw the utility in claiming that I was trying to conceal or advocate for public record destruction since he was trying to keep me out of the DOJ. I had been complaining about his handling of the Lincoln Hills investigation for months, and it would come out later that he really wanted to appoint his friend and transition director into my civil service position as DCI administrator. And I'm sure the governor's office also saw the utility. Not only had two cabinet secretaries come forward saying that they had been instructed not to make records, but also for the past year, Walker had been waging an expensive battle not to release the emails from his office concerning a drastic rewriting of the "Wisconsin Idea." Ironically, the Walker administration had claimed that those emails were merely drafts and therefore not subject to the open records law. And in Zipperer's letter to me, he acknowledged that the documents I wanted to deliver to his office and ultimately sent to him were known to be drafts, because I had told him so prior to sending them. Oops.

When I received Zipperer's letter of admonishment in response to my letter and draft document, I called and left him a voicemail message. I explained again that the letter I sent was a draft, and he knew that because we had spoken prior to me sending it. He never returned my call. Instead, he contacted Katie Ignatowski, the governor's legal chief and wife of the governor's aide who had been notified about Lincoln Hills years before, to advise her that I had mailed him the note and draft document. Katie, in turn, would then send those documents to the DOJ by email, but only after Deputy Attorney General Andy Cook was called over to Zipperer's office to see the letter before it was sent. They were not trying to help right the wrongs; they were in fact lining up the gun sights to deliver the coup de grâce. You see, the governor's office could have held my letter and draft as a record, and it would have remained there unless someone requested a copy pursuant to an open records response. But they took the highly unusual step of making it an open record by sending me a letter and email. It was orchestrated; it was all theater.

In the meantime, I continued to revise my draft transfer appeal to the Wisconsin Employment Relations Commission. I carefully described all the background and laid out my case. In summary, I said that my reassignment was executed contrary to law and state personnel administrative rules without explanation. Effectively, the move violated the laws concerning restoration from the unclassified service, and the reassignment constituted a constructive demotion without just cause or due process that negatively affected me, my family, my retirement benefits, and my reputation, and removed me from my 30-plus-year law enforcement career.

The day after receiving Zipperer's letter, I went to Florida for a pre-planned family vacation. We were badly in need of a little respite from the agonizing knothole that the DOJ was pulling us through. I had already been to the doctor a few times for chest pain, panic attacks, and inability to sleep. Reluctantly, I let my doctor put me on anxiety medications, and he had given me other pills to help me sleep. I didn't want to take medications to deal with the problems these politicians were causing because I saw it as just another surrender I would be making to them. There is nothing I love more on this earth than my family, and it was only after my wife begged me to let the doctor help that I acquiesced.

Our vacation to Florida was unfortunately anything but relaxing, and the DOJ would see to it that the stress continued. I had sent an email to Connell, who was then my immediate supervisor, prior to going to Florida to request the time off. Although I was on administrative leave, I didn't want to give them anything to wrap around my neck if I left the state while I was on leave. Connell sent me back a note telling me to enjoy my time with the family.

We were in Florida just a few days, and I was trying to play a game of golf with a friend. It was very windy that day, and when my phone rang, I almost didn't hear it. When I answered, I heard Paul Connell, and he stated that there was someone else on the line as well. My stomach immediately sunk because I knew this was another one of Connell's cowardly ambush tactics. Connell was saying something about sending me an email and text message, but I had no idea what he was talking about.

He then asked me if I sent a letter and document to Rich Zipperer at his residence, and I replied that I had. It was at that moment I realized Zipperer had sent the letter and draft document to the DOJ. There was no obligation for the governor's office to turn those documents over to the DOJ, so there could only be one reason they did; Zipperer wanted to permanently end my restoration issues and sever me from the governor by creating a record and a story around it.

Connell advised that I would be receiving a pre-disciplinary letter, and I immediately asked, "For what?" Connell would not answer and only said that it would be explained in the pre-disciplinary letter. I was devastated. I had never been the subject of a disciplinary action in my 32 years as a public servant, and now I had this political appointee trying to end my career.

I said to Connell, "Paul, why are you doing this to me?" and he hung up. What I did not know was that this ambush call would constitute the entire DOJ investigation into my letter and circumstances.

When state employees are going to be interviewed for disciplinary actions, they have to be advised in advance of any investigative interview, and they are also to be advised they have the right to have legal counsel or a representative with them at the time of that interview. If the information can be used against them in future proceedings, then they must be advised of their rights prior to any questioning, very similar to the rights people have in law enforcement investigations.

Connell never contacted me to advise me that he wished to interview me regarding a disciplinary issue. When he reached me on the golf course, he did not alert me that he was conducting an interview concerning a disciplinary action. Yes, he had tried to send me a text message and an email earlier in the day, but when I returned from the golf course, the text and email that I found on my iPad simply said he wished to speak with me. That evening, Connell did send me a pre-disciplinary letter signed by the human resources director but written by Connell by his own admission in depositions later.

March 16, 2016

Mr. Edward Wall
6672 Highland Drive
Windsor, WI 53598

Dear Mr. Wall,

This letter is to notify you that a pre-disciplinary meeting is scheduled for March 17, 2016, at 3 p.m. (Central Time) in Room 150A, of the Risser Justice Center. Given the significance of the allegations set forth below, we are unwilling to delay this matter. We will allot up to one and one-half hours for this meeting. Since you are out of state, you may participate by phone. The meeting will be conducted by me and also attended by Senior Counsel Paul Connell and DLS Administrator David Meany. You will be provided the telephone number and passcode shortly before the meeting. Please note that the sole basis for the investigation, this letter, the pre-disciplinary hearing, and any subsequent discipline imposed are certain statements in the letter sent by you on March 10, 2016, and the manner in which you sent it, to Rich Zipperer, Chief of Staff to the Governor, which is referenced below. Neither the attachment to that letter or any references to a possible civil service complaint in that letter are being taken into consideration.

This meeting is your opportunity to provide any mitigating evidence or additional information you want the Department of Justice to consider before issuing a final disposition regarding any potential disciplinary action taken against you, which may include termination. You are entitled to have a personal representative attend this meeting. He or she may attend in person or via phone. The role of the representative is to assist you in presenting your information. No weapons or recording devices will be allowed at the meeting if anyone attends on your behalf.

After a thorough investigation including the investigatory meeting held with you on March 15, 2016, via phone and a review of the results, the department has concluded you have violated the following Wisconsin Department of Justice Work Rules and DCI policies and procedures.

DOJ Work Rules

1. Insubordination, disobedience, or refusal to carry out written or verbal assignments, directions, or instructions.

4. Unauthorized use of confidential information.

9. Failure to comply with Department policies, rules and regulations.

20. Making false or malicious statements concerning other employees, supervisors or the Department.

32. Failure to exercise good judgment, or being discourteous, in dealing with fellow employees, supervisors, or the public, or other behaviors unbecoming of a state employee.

Policy 100 Rules of Conduct

IIA2 All agents and analysts are required to establish and maintain a working knowledge of all state laws which they have the authority to enforce. They must adhere to the policies and procedures of the Department and the Division and are responsible for keeping abreast of all new or modified policies or procedures. In the event of improper action or breach of discipline, it will be presumed that the agent or analyst was familiar with the law, rule or policy in question.

IIA5 No agent or analyst shall engage in any conduct that would reflect unfavorably on Wisconsin state government.

The Department has concluded that you violated the above work rules and DCI policies by sending a letter to the Governor's Chief of Staff, Rich Zipperer, on March 10, 2016, at his home address. The letter called into question the authority of the Attorney General and made false accusations regarding your direct supervisor and another member of the Attorney General's Executive Staff. By sending the letter to Mr. Zipperer at his home address you knowingly attempted, and encouraged the Governor's Chief of Staff, to evade and violate Wisconsin's public records laws. Furthermore, in that letter you also encouraged Mr. Zipperer to evade and violate the Governor's Office own internal policies and procedures related to records retention. In fact, you specifically invited Mr. Zipperer to shred the letter and attachment once he had looked it over.

As a reminder, the Department has an Employee Assistance Program that can assist you in addressing any problems that may be impacting you. You can contact LifeMatters at 1-800-634-6433 or visit their website at mylifematters.com. Last, since you are currently on vacation, the time spent by you during the pre-disciplinary hearing will be credited back to your leave account.

Sincerely,
Jayne Swingen
Human Resources Director
Human Resources Bureau

Terminated? I wrote a private note to my past supervisor out of desperation, and I might be terminated? Although the letter refers to the "investigatory meeting" Connell had with me, the meeting was without notice, I was not given advisement of right to counsel, and I was asked a single question that I gave a one-word answer to. Additionally, the letter said, "The department has concluded you violated the above ..." before ever hearing from me.

I was also stunned that the letter said I was to have a pre-disciplinary meeting *the following day*, although I was on vacation in Florida with my family. I replied that I was concerned that they were rushing the process. I also stated that I was concerned that they had apparently conducted an investigatory interview where I was not given advance notice or advised of my right to counsel. Further, I advised them that I was on approved vacation out of state with my family and did not have any of the documents they would be referring to in a pre-disciplinary meeting. I asked that they postpone this pre-disciplinary meeting, and I told them I wished to speak with an attorney.

Connell replied by sending me copies of my letter and draft appeal document that I had sent to Zipperer. The real reason he sent them was to create a record with the documents attached so that he could justify releasing it to the press a short time later. He further stated that he was not inclined to grant my request to postpone the pre-disciplinary meeting but would review it and advise me later. The next morning, the DOJ Human Resources director sent me an email advising that the meeting would be postponed until the day after I returned from vacation with my family.

I immediately called my friend, Attorney Dan Bach, the former deputy attorney general under Peg Lautenschlager. I explained what they were doing, and Dan agreed to help me out. I forwarded him the documents Connell had sent to me, and we agreed to meet the morning of the pre-disciplinary hearing.

On the day we were returning home from our vacation, I received a call while in the airport. It was *Milwaukee Journal Sentinel* reporter Jason Stein, who called wanting to know if I had any comment on the records that the DOJ had just released to the press. I had no idea what he was referring to and asked, "What records?" Stein advised me that the DOJ released my letter to Zipperer and my attached draft appeal document.

I told Stein I had no comment and hung up the phone. Another panic attack ensued. The DOJ was launching a smear campaign against me and was making sure that they rallied public support for the actions they had intended from the start. As if their intentional attempts to play fast and loose with the state personnel laws and policies were not enough, they were now violating my rights under the state open records law—*the very law they were alleging I tried to avoid.*

Following are the relevant parts of that law:

OPEN RECORDS LAW: WISCONSIN STATE STATUTE 19.356(2)(A)(1):

*Except as provided in pars. (b) to (d) and as otherwise authorized or required by statute, if an authority decides under s. 19.35 to permit access to a record specified in this paragraph, **the authority shall, before permitting access and within 3 days after making the decision to permit access, serve*** *written notice of that decision on any record subject to whom the record pertains, either by certified mail or by personally serving the notice on the record subject. The notice shall briefly describe the requested record and include a description of the rights of the record subject under subs. (3) and (4). This paragraph applies only to the following records:*

1. A record containing information relating to an employee that is created or kept by the authority and that is the result of an investigation into a disciplinary matter involving the employee or possible employment-related violation by the employee of a statute, ordinance, rule, regulation, or policy of the employee's employer.

WISCONSIN STATE STATUTE 19.36(10)(B):

*EMPLOYEE PERSONNEL RECORDS. Unless access is specifically authorized or required by statute, **an authority shall not provide access** under s. 19.35 (1) **to records containing the following information**, except to an employee or the employee's representative to the extent required under s. 103.13 or to a recognized or certified collective bargaining representative to the extent required to fulfill a duty to bargain under ch. 111 or pursuant to a collective bargaining agreement under ch. 111:*

Information relating to the current investigation of a possible criminal offense or possible misconduct connected with employment by an employee prior to disposition of the investigation.

The wording in the open records statutes is not ambiguous. The DOJ was *required* by state law to give me advance notice of its intent to release my employee records so that I could contest that decision in court if I elected to do so. Additionally, the law specifically prohibited the release of documents pertaining to a personnel investigation before the investigation was completed. Obviously, the investigation wasn't completed because I had not even had my pre-disciplinary hearing to offer my own information. In essence, the state's top law enforcement official, the attorney general, was making vague assertions that I had *suggested* to someone that they could *evade* the public records law while Schimel and his minions actively violated that same law twice in furtherance of his efforts to end my career. What they were engaging in was nothing less than character assassination.

I called Dan Bach and advised him that the DOJ had released the information, and he was equally as stunned as I was. He agreed that this appeared to be a premeditated attempt to destroy my credibility, knowing that I had criticized their failure in the Lincoln Hills investigation. When Dan and I met the morning of the pre-disciplinary hearing, he was also convinced that the DOJ was simply going through the steps to terminate me, even though they were doing it all wrong.

When we entered the meeting, there was the DOJ Human Resources director, who had been put up to run the meeting to give it an air of proper state agency process. DOJ Administrator of Legal Services Dave Meany was present—the same person I had spoken with and warned after the meeting with the Milwaukee juvenile judge and the horrible briefing by the DOJ. Also attending was Delaney Brewer, another attorney with a title I don't recall, and Corey Finkelmeyer, a staff assistant attorney general I had known for years. I considered Corey a friend and would have never guessed that he would have condoned what was happening, but I came to realize he was just answering to his handlers and had to place his ethics on the shelf—something I could never do.

Dan opened the meeting by advising those present that the pre-disciplinary letter gave absolutely no information concerning the actions I had supposedly taken with regard to the work rule violations I was being accused of. It only listed work rules and policies without any context for each accusation. Dan asked the DOJ to please go through the charges and let us know what actions I had taken that constituted the supposed violations so that we could answer them. Corey then announced, "We are not here to answer your questions; we are here to listen to any information you may have that you want taken into consideration before we make a decision." That comment pretty much stole the oxygen out of the room, as they refused to even identify what actions I took that violated work rules. Besides, they had already stated in their pre-disciplinary letter that they *had determined* my guilt before hearing from me.

Dan pointed out that the DOJ did not give me advance notice of an investigative interview when they called me on my approved vacation with my family out of state. Then he pointed out that I had not been advised of my rights to counsel or a representative before Connell asked the single question that would constitute his investigation.

I was then allowed to talk about what was happening and why. I apologized for the letter, admitted it was the biggest mistake of my life, and explained that the DOJ had pushed me to the most desperate place I had ever been in my career. I explained that I had never had any training in open records and simply wanted to get the reluctant chief of staff to take notice that one of the governor's appointees was being denied his statutorily protected civil service position by those who were now in charge of his home agency. They sat stone-faced and did not ask any questions.

Dan closed the meeting by pointing out that I had a spotless 32-year career in law enforcement, had been asked to lead three state agencies by Democratic and Republican governors and a Republican attorney general, and had earned my DCI administrator position through a civil service process. He asked that they consider taking corrective action if they thought my understanding of the public record laws could be improved but did not feel that this required any type of severe disciplinary action. We parted after polite handshakes.

Dan sent a letter to Finkelmeyer after the meeting outlining the issues we raised and noting that there were issues of great concern with regard to due process and just cause. Dan again pointed out that I was not advised, as required by law, that I could have a representative or legal counsel present when I was being interviewed over the phone about the disciplinary matter. He pointed out that my letter and a draft of my appeal were released from my file without notifying me or offering me an opportunity to object, as required by law. And then he rebutted, point by point, each of the allegations against me.

A few days went by, and on Friday, April 8, 2016, Dan called me at home and advised that the DOJ had reached out to him and wanted to talk with him the following Tuesday about my case. We both were hopeful that they would want to discuss a settlement and end this nightmare. That was wishful thinking.

Dan called me the afternoon of April 12 and advised that the DOJ said that either we reach a "negotiated disposition" or I would be terminated on Friday, April 15. We made several offers to the DOJ on compromises, and each one was turned away. Finally, they said that I could take a demotion to a special agent position, and if I didn't resign within 90 days, they would terminate me. That was not an offer; it was blackmail. The DOJ was counting on me running away to preserve my 2,000-plus hours of accumulated sick time that I had earned over 16 years by not using a single sick day. I could not bring myself to resign and run after what these politicians were doing to me. I had not done anything wrong beyond desperately trying to save my 32-year law enforcement career from political assassins. ♠

DARKEST BEFORE
THE DAWN

On Friday, April 15, 2016, I received an emailed termination letter. The panic attacks ensued. My stomach started to turn, my fingers were tingling, and I broke into a cold sweat. I began to cry and held my head in my hands. What had I done to deserve this? I questioned my faith. I was filled with anger, hatred, fear, humiliation, and panic.

The news of my termination was plastered across the newspapers statewide. I was so embarrassed, so hurt. I feared for what my family would go through, and I was voiceless. The press was ravenous, and the DOJ naturally played to it with Schimel making the statement:

"Unfortunately, I lost confidence with Mr. Wall and determined he could no longer serve in any capacity at the DOJ after learning that he directed a high-ranking state official to shred public records."

Schimel knew very well that I had not "directed" anyone to do anything, but it served to prosecute his case against me from his bully pulpit as the attorney general. His staff admitted in deposition that I had not "directed" anyone to shred documents. The governor's chief of staff stated that he did not feel he was directed to do anything.

But the public statement was made, and you can't get the toothpaste back in the tube. Schimel's statement was nothing short of defamation, slander, and libel, and it will follow me the rest of my life. If we could afford an attorney, we would file suit based on his intentional misleading statement that was published across the state.

Schimel knew that I was nothing more than a desperate man who did not want his career ended for no reason—a career my family and I had sacrificed so much for. By intentionally twisting my desperate pleas for help into something he wanted to look like veiled violations of law, he had succeeded in convicting me in the court of public opinion without so much as a trial or the truth. Besides that, he made it clear in that statement that he felt I somehow had to have his confidence to maintain my civil service position. He would repeatedly misconstrue the meaning of civil service and the fact that his "confidence" had nothing to do with a classified civil servant job.

I fled to our cabin that weekend to disappear, and my wife and kids would be coming up later that evening to join me. I was beyond devastated. Never in my career had I ever been disciplined in the slightest, let alone terminated. My career was destroyed, my credibility ruined, my family exposed to embarrassment, and I could not see tomorrow. As the day progressed, my panic attacks intensified. I could not hold down food, and I felt physically weak. I would just start to cry, sobbing until my chest hurt. My wife called later and said that she wasn't going to get up there that night as planned but would be up in the morning, and I told her that was okay. I was tired and needed sleep.

I hung up the phone and started to cry again. I was 55 years old and now unemployed due to two devious, calculating politicians and their henchmen. My head was swimming, my knees weak, the room was moving around me, and I went into our bedroom to lie down. As I entered the bedroom, I glanced over and saw my computer bag sitting on the dresser. I stepped over and opened the bag. I looked inside at my handgun—the same gun I had carried for years to protect the public, the gun that was often a source of comfort as danger lurked all around me. The agony was more than I could bear, and that gun, that once trusted companion, was now staring at me. It seemed to be an answer to the pain and anger I couldn't stand any longer.

I put my hand on the gun and slowly pulled it out. The weight in my hand seemed to drive home what was going through my mind. I sat at the foot of the bed with shoulders slumped, my chest heaving with gasps for air as I felt the effects of hyperventilation coming on. Sobbing uncontrollably, I stared at that gun and felt only anger. I wanted Walker, Zipperer, Schimel, and Connell to know how badly they had hurt me and my family. I wanted their dishonesty, their deceit, their injustice, their unethical actions, to burn in their souls for the rest of their lives. They needed to know that their actions had consequences, and this was the way to drive that point home.

As I raised the gun up, the barrel grew in size. It was all happening so slowly. My fingers began to tingle, and I could feel my fine motor skills abandoning me as I hyperventilated, sobbing. Tunnel vision shrunk my focal point, as I opened my mouth and slowly put the gun inside. This was it; this was the end. I would make them pay. It was time to end the pain. Maybe next time, they would stop and think about ruining people's lives. I couldn't take it anymore. They won. My teeth were chattering against the slide of my pistol as I shook. It was so surreal, the taste of the bittersweet gun oil and the odd sensation of the cold metal against my tongue and the roof of my mouth. I was conscious of my finger tightening on the trigger, and so many things were flashing in front of me. The memories, the faces, were like a deck of shuffling cards, and suddenly one of those visions froze in front of me.

It was Craig Klyve, my former supervisor and close friend who had taken his own life. Was this what it was like for him? Was the agony and despair the same? What were his final thoughts? And my own words started ringing in my ears: "If only I had been able to talk to him for two minutes, I know I could have stopped him." But my hand kept tightening on the gun, and I pressed it harder against the roof of my mouth, pushing until the gun broke the skin. Then my mind suddenly flashed to my wife and children. They would be the ones to find what was left of their husband and father.

I remember thinking, "What would Debi say to me if she was here right now, if she had the same two minutes I didn't have with Craig?"

She would say, "Don't do this. We love you, and they don't matter. Don't let them win. Don't sacrifice us for them. They are not worth it."

I had two voices screaming in my head, one telling me, "Do it. Pull the trigger. Let those bastards pay the price for your sacrifice." The other voice was measured, calm, reasonable, and said, "You know better than this. These people are not worth your life, and your family will be the only ones paying the price. Nothing means more to you than your family."

My grip started to ease. Reason overcame pain and anger as I let my hand with the gun drop to my lap, cognizant of the pain on the roof of my mouth and the taste of blood. I stared at the gun and became angry with myself for even considering what I had just come so close to doing. I had been the one to try and effect changes in suicide awareness and prevention, to help others see there was another choice, yet there I was on the precipice of mortality by my own actions. The gun slipped from my fingers and fell to the floor as I fell back on the bed and just cried. I was ashamed and embarrassed at being so weak, but my soul now understood what could bring people to the point of no return.

It was a long night of sleeplessness. Our problems always seem so much worse at night, racing between thoughts as logical answers evade the subconscious. The next morning, I drove home, calling my wife to tell her I was on my way back. When I hung up, I said out loud in my car, "Thank you, God, for pulling me back, and thank you, Craig, for stepping in to save me when I could not save you." I started crying again, still upset with myself for letting my anger over a two-faced governor and deceitful attorney general drive me to the brink of self-destruction.

It occurred to me on my drive home that they would probably have been happy and relieved if I had pulled that trigger. They would have likely said that I had something to hide and the public would have been left with yet another erroneous vision of me in their minds—all carefully crafted by politicians skilled in the art of cover-up and story changing.

As I have found since that fateful day, you never forget the taste of a gun in your mouth. No matter how hard you try, it is burned in your memory along with the cascade of events that brought you to the edge of destruction. It haunts you, and there has not been a day since that I haven't woken up thinking about it. However, if you are fortunate enough that God steps in and lifts you past that chasm of despair, a stronger person can rise from the ashes, forged in determination. But it takes time.

When I returned home, I talked with my wife and again broke down, telling her what I had almost done and apologizing for being so weak and selfish that I would even consider leaving her and our children. She did as she always did and just held me in her arms and assured me that I did nothing wrong. We both knew I needed to speak with someone to get a hold of my emotions and the rapid unraveling of my life. I called my doctor, and he had me come right in. I described the repeated panic attacks I had been having for weeks, and he watched with pain in his eyes as I again broke down in tears, trying to explain what I was feeling. I was scared, defeated, physically ill, and worried that I would not be able to find work to support my family after this campaign of false information.

For my entire life, I was the bedrock for my family and friends. Strong, confident, compassionate, and inspired. Now I just wanted to disappear. I was paranoid that everyone was looking at me and viewing me as a lawbreaker and dirty public servant because of what two politicians had painted for the public to see, just to protect themselves.

My doctor sent me to speak with a psychologist, who I would subsequently meet with a number of times. Admittedly, deep down inside, I did not want to go. In my mind, it was a sign of weakness that I could not deal with my own problems. That's not what cops do; we fix problems. We are strong in the face of adversity. We persevere. We don't rely on others; they rely on us. Unfortunately, the agonizing truth was, at that point in my life, I couldn't even rely on myself to think clearly. I would wake up in the morning and curl up in the fetal position, immobilized by fear. I didn't want to leave the house. How would I support my family? How would I pay for an attorney? Would we lose our home? What about health insurance, which we needed so desperately with Emily's hydrocephalus? I had so many questions, and for the first time in my life, I had no answers. I had no plan.

It was during my appointments with my psychologist that he was able to make me understand one thing: I had done nothing wrong. My family and friends had repeatedly told me that, but they were supposed to do that. The doctor, on the other hand, was a neutral and detached listening post and broke down my situation into its simplest terms. I had been intentionally pushed by *unethical* people to the point of collapse so that they could fulfill their own agenda. That was the bottom line, and the word *unethical* wouldn't leave my mind because that one word captured exactly what they were to me and in reality. He recommended that I stop several times a day and look at myself in the mirror and say, "You did nothing wrong." And he was right. Slowly, very slowly, my depression, anxiety, and fear turned into something else. It went from black to gray and from gray to opaque. The world started to turn warmer. But it seemed happiness would never be the same.

One of the more painful aspects of the entire nightmare was being abandoned by some of the people I thought were my friends. What I soon came to realize was that they were really just acquaintances, because friends don't walk away when there are storm clouds on the horizon. Friends offer to help brace you for the coming weather, help hold your course through the thick of it and help repair the damage afterward. I was blessed with some wonderful friends. The others just drifted away like a herd of gazelles when one of their own is injured and the lions are stalking nearby. Nobody wants to be the next meal. It would have been a blessing just to hear their voices, but the silence was deafening. It was like those relationships never existed, and you would think I would have washed my hands and walked away. But I still miss them.

Once you have been at the very bottom, only then can you truly appreciate the new dawn and the warmth of the sun on your face. The medications began to take effect after a few weeks, and my life started to move, ever so slowly, forward. I went for walks and would sit for long periods in the chairs in our garden, just looking around and absorbing the air, the sun, the birds. I was taking in life with a new respect for the gift that it was, and I knew I would have been missing all of this if I had followed through with a short stroke of my finger.

I would often close my eyes with our little dog, Gracie, sitting faithfully by my side on our front steps and let the sun warm my face. I will never forget the tingle down my spine as my wife would walk up behind me and put her hand on my shoulder. All the things I came so close to letting go of were now the things I cherished the most—such simple things, yet their extraordinary meaning had slipped past me in my years of haste to serve. My wife had warned me many times over the years that, at the end of the career I cherished so much, only she and the kids would still be there, waiting to take in what was left of my battered body and soul that I had given so willingly to serve others. She was absolutely right; I had allowed my priorities to become twisted. The sacrifices my family had endured throughout my career were immense, yet I nearly let the end of that career send them down the path of perpetual suffering by pulling a trigger. That would never happen again. The disappointment with myself for letting my anger nearly stop me from seeing my family and the beauty of life slowly receded. It will, however, live with me always. 🐾

LESSONS LEARNED

On my last day at the DOC, the governor called to thank me for my service. He told me that he knew I did my best and appreciated all the personal effort I had put into trying to address Lincoln Hills. That was it—a phone call. Three and a half years of dedication, commitment, sacrifice, sweat, tears, and exhausting work, and it ended with a phone call. Why just a phone call? Because a letter telling me what he said would become a record, and they couldn't have that. They needed to change the story and put in a new face so they could claim progress, even though they had been given the roadmap to improvements over two years earlier. Besides, you can't be seen publicly thanking the guy who you and the attorney general intended to malign.

Throughout my life, I have always looked at times of stress and peril as opportunities to learn. Not generally during the events, but certainly after. If you go through trying times and you don't learn anything, then the experience is wasted. Even though two unethical politicians ultimately destroyed my public service career, the experience of that career was not wasted. Regardless of their determination to paint me as something I was not, they could not erase the good things that had happened during my public safety service. They do not understand the drive, commitment, and dedication that people in public safety professions live for. We are not driven by a desire to acquire power or accolades, but rather to help others.

Scott Walker and Brad Schimel both had me convinced that they were perhaps something other than selfish politicians who would do and say anything to gain power and hang on to it in their drive for higher offices. Even though I thought I had mastered the job of judging people when I was a cop, I was wrong. I had misjudged them badly.

My service to the public was unblemished before they came into my life. I had been decorated for bravery, heroism, saving lives, apprehending criminals, and exemplary service to the citizens I served in three states. Governors and attorneys general of both parties had asked me to lead three of the state's most critical public safety agencies, and not because of political connections, because I had none. Rather, they had heard about and seen my work ethic and determination. I had not so much as a written reprimand in three decades. The sacrifices that my family and I made for my career cannot be calculated in dollars, hours, or benefits. They can only be calculated in tears, which ended up being a very high price.

For over 32 years, I toiled through positions of ever-increasing responsibilities with one intention only: to respond and help. Be the first to run to the scene when the alarms sound, when the shots are fired, when the call for help goes out. It is a driving force that only those who have entered into emergency service work can understand. Scott Walker and Brad Schimel have never exhibited that kind of drive, compassion, and desire to serve. That is why they will never understand the damage they did to me, my family, and government employees across the state. They bastardized the laws that protect civil servants, leaving devastated lives in their path.

They stripped my family of over 2,000 hours of *earned* sick time that was meant to pay for our health insurance when I would eventually retire. I used vacation and personal time for my sick days and never once took a sick day in 16 years of service to the state of Wisconsin, trying to save that time for the future. Now it is all gone because I stood my ground. It was a heavy price to pay.

Ultimately, we spent $100,000 in legal fees to challenge my termination. We had a mountain of evidence on our side. First, I filed an appeal to the Wisconsin Employment Relations Commission that I'd been illegally forced from my position and constructively demoted by DOJ. The WERC is composed of three political appointees of the governor, who was the same guy that wanted me and my issues to disappear. We appealed their ruling against me in court, but we found that the court was required to give great deference to the WERC decision, and the judge would never hear from me at all. In fact, the only people who could judge my credibility were the governor's appointees. There would be no unbiased judgment by anyone in my case. Lastly, we filed an appeal with the Wisconsin Department of Workforce Development, and an equal rights officer at Workforce Development found there was probable cause that I'd been illegally retaliated against. But then it was ruled by a Department of Workforce Development administrative law judge, in one of the governor's cabinet agencies, that Wisconsin's whistleblower law didn't cover cabinet secretaries, even though I was a classified civil servant on approved leave to serve the governor. In all, the entire process of appeal was controlled from the beginning by people who answered to the politicians who wanted me gone. There was no fair and impartial hearing, no jury of my peers. It was shameful.

Unfortunately, I did not find justice. But in the process, I found out a lot about myself.

While Walker and Schimel did their best to destroy my credibility, reputation, and employability, the people who actually know me are well aware of who and what I am. I speak the truth. I will always lend a helping hand. I am driven by dogged determination. I love without limitation, and I keep my word. If you are a friend, I am always there for you. The reality is that the picture these two unethical politicians tried to paint is more reflective of who they are: immoral, deceitful, dishonest, and manipulative. They do not abide by a sense of common decency. Their only concern is staying in power and placating big-money donors who work their strings like puppeteers. Party before everything.

Hopefully, someday Walker and Schimel will understand that their actions as politicians have real-world impacts on those they represent and those they employ. It's not all about which donor is going to give them money. It's not all about the next campaign, the next legislative battle to gain votes, or higher political office. It's about doing what is morally and ethically right, not always what is popular. It's not about polls; it's about living a good and honest life.

My entire life, I have been a faithful Christian. To listen to the governor and the attorney general, they would have you believe that they also are true to their faith. It is popular to appeal to people with a faith connection and call attention to your beliefs because that could get you votes. But there is a big difference between saying what is right and doing what is right. There is a big difference between *being* Christian and *doing* Christian. Knowing the difference is often the key to who you really are and how you lead your life.

With that, I must give credit where credit is due. Walker and Schimel taught me the most valuable lesson of all: Life is the most precious gift that God has given each of us. It's not to be taken for granted or cast aside because the fear of the moment clouds the future. Fear, anxiety, pain, and panic are momentary in the big picture. To this day, I am embarrassed and angry with myself that these two unworthy men were able to bring me to the brink of self-destruction. But I persevered, in spite of them.

For those who have found themselves in places of bottomless depression and gloom, know that you are not alone. I could never understand the thought process surrounding suicide until I found myself staring it in the face. It is not something you can explain to others. So, please trust me, no matter what you feel when you are in that dark place, where nothing seems to make sense except ending the pain—STOP. In each of our lives, there is hope and love that can be overshadowed to the point that we can't see it or even remember it, but it is there. Don't be afraid to ask for help, no matter how strong you think you are. Find a person that cares about you and ask them, "What would your life be like if I was gone?" Then listen to the answer. Focus on those thoughts. Feel the hope and love.

Behind that veil of darkness, just beyond where you can see at that moment, there is a sunrise. There is warmth, love, purpose, and help. Just think about the people who love you the most and ask yourself, "What would they say to me if they had just two minutes to talk to me?" They would tell you they love you. They would tell you not to destroy yourself. They would tell you it gets better. And they would be right. You owe it to them, and you owe it to yourself, to listen to that message. The essence of life is love, and love is there for you, even at the deepest levels of despair.

Conversely, if you know someone who you fear is walking down that path themselves, talk to them and don't be afraid to ask them if they are thinking about self-harm. That simple inquiry can be the string that pulls them away from the edge. Get them help any way possible, show them compassion at any cost, because you may be the only angel they have at that moment.

Today I am working out of state. My family remains in Wisconsin, and I travel home every few weeks to see them. The separation is very difficult, but required, since finding a job in Wisconsin was so adversely affected by all of the bad press generated by Walker and Schimel. I have been turned down time and again for positions in Wisconsin I was overqualified for, but someday I hope to return to a position in service to others, back in the Badger State with my family.

Lastly, the most difficult lesson that I had to learn involved forgiveness. My faith teaches me that if I am to have my own trespasses forgiven, then I must be willing to forgive those who have trespassed against me. So, you should know that I have forgiven Scott Walker, Brad Schimel, Rich Zipperer, Paul Connell, and their staffs, praying that they take the time in the future to consider their actions and the effect they will have on other people's lives. You see, forgiveness is not about forgetting about what has happened or erasing the past. It also doesn't mean that the people you forgive are going to change their ways. It simply involves letting go of the hurt, pain, and anger to move on with your own life.

I have let all that go, because ultimately, this book was an exercise in therapy, forgiveness and simply telling the truth that was never told. My family and I have moved on from the ordeal with unethical politicians. I am blessed that my wife, children, and true friends have shown me unbridled, never-ending love, for which I am forever grateful. Life is good. God bless. ♦

AFTERWORD

Toward the end of 2017, the press became aware that I was writing this book, and reporters called and interviewed me. I confirmed the rumors and revealed a few details, especially about how Walker and Schimel mishandled the problems at Lincoln Hills and manipulated my employment issues.

Mere days later, Walker decided that he would push to close down Lincoln Hills and take action on plans I had recommended over two and a half years before. The legislature that had time and again turned away the DOC and their requests for funding to address the festering issues of Corrections now raced to throw money at the problems. My phone rang for days as media outlets asked if I thought this turnaround was because of my book. I'll never know for sure, but if all that was accomplished by writing this book was that it might have helped force politicians to finally address the need for corrections reforms, or more importantly, caused one suicidal person to step back from the brink and give life a chance, then it was all worthwhile.

Ultimately, the governor and legislature did pass legislation to close Lincoln Hills and work toward the regionalized plan my administration had recommended in the fall of 2015. On the day before that the bill was passed, the state settled one of the many Lincoln Hills lawsuits filed against them for nearly $19 million. It's the largest state agency settlement in Wisconsin history and about one quarter of the cost estimate to implement the *entire* juvenile corrections reform bill. Ultimately, Zipperer was right. Walker and the legislature would not take action until they were sued, and the state would pay millions for their refusal to act. And the investigation I requested the DOJ to conduct is still not closed after nearly four years. Maybe after the election ...

As the publicity about my book grew, Walker and Schimel's attempts to malign me would grow also. Schimel and his minions would lean on the "disgruntled employee" crutch, still alluding to open records issues. The governor wouldn't directly comment but did what he usually did and referred it to someone else, the Wisconsin Republican Party. They would make the false accusation that I had "secretly lobbied for another job," which was an outright lie. I simply wanted the job back that was guaranteed by law—law that a governor and attorney general saw as something they could change at their whim. Civil servants who might accept political appointments should keep that in mind.

Finally, as I am about to deliver this book to the publisher, the Wisconsin DOC is now on its fourth secretary under Walker's term. That is a state record that doesn't speak to the agency, but to the governor's lack of concern and unwillingness to address problems until forced to do so at election time. That is not leadership; it is self-preservation at any cost.

Wisconsin deserves better. Wisconsin deserves leaders. 🐾

To see more documentation and unpublished information, please visit: UNETHICALBOOK.com

ABOUT THE AUTHOR

Ed Wall was a 32-year career public safety professional, having served as a police officer in Meriden, Connecticut, a state trooper in New Hampshire, and a special agent and then special agent in charge of the Wisconsin Division of Criminal Investigation, before he became administrator of that division.

Additionally, Ed was appointed by Democratic Governor Jim Doyle as the administrator of Wisconsin Emergency Management and was later appointed cabinet secretary of the Wisconsin Department of Corrections by Republican Governor Scott Walker.

Ed has been married to his wife, Debi, since 1990, and they have three children: Caitlin, Emily, and Ryan. ❦